THE SECRET STAITHES DIARY

of
Enid Lucy Pease Robinson

Selected and Edited by
James Hart

Historical Publishing

1

This edition published in 2010 by Historical Publishing
Copyright © 2010 Historical Publishing

Printed in Great Britain by G H Smith, Easingwold, York

Selected and edited by James Hart
Art Direction and design by John Haxby

Front cover image: 'The Lookout' by Robert Jobling,
courtesy of Walker Galleries, Harrogate (Private Collection)

Rear cover image: 'The Old Trestle Bridge at Staithes – 1902'
by John Bowman (Private Collection)

ISBN 978-0-9565317-0-4

For further information visit www.historicalpublishing.co.uk
or e-mail: info@historicalpublishing.co.uk

Enid Lucy Pease Robinson circa 1900

In memory of Enid Lucy Pease Robinson
(*later* Steavenson)

6th August 1881 ~ 1975

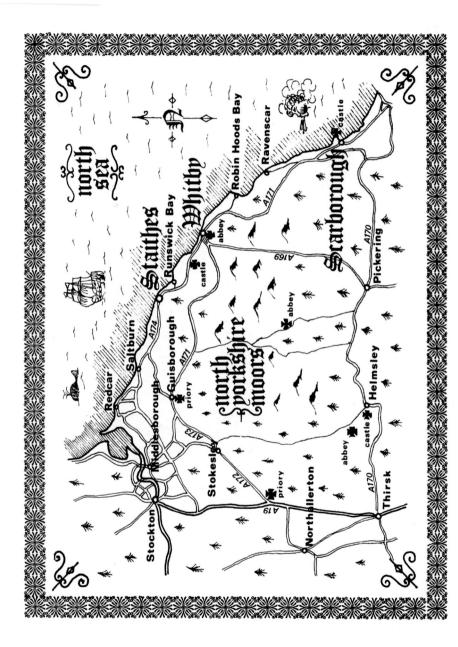

Enid Lucy Pease Robinson circa 1901

Better to write for yourself and have no public,
than to write for the public and have no self.

– Cyril Connolly (1903~74) –

It is not a bad idea to get in the habit of writing down one's
thoughts. It saves one having to bother anyone else with them.

– Isabel Colegate –

Lucy Ann Pease ~ 1862
Born 1844 ~ Died 1911

Foreword by Honor Pullen

I am Honor Theresa Pullen, the youngest daughter of Enid Lucy Pease Steavenson (née Robinson).

James Hart cleverly discovered my identity and whereabouts and I was delighted to receive a copy of the diary you are about to read. Although, this is unmistakably my mother's diary, I have no recollection of ever seeing or reading it, although I do still possess many of her drawings, poetry, diaries and journals. My mother loved visiting Staithes in her younger days, and then as children we had many family outings there, our home; Middleton St George, Darlington being only about 22 miles away.

My Mother wrote an amusing poem when she was aged only sixteen. It was about her daydreams, and how she would like her life to unfold. It turned out to be very prophetic, as she did go on to have four children, a boy, girl, boy and girl (me).

Before my mother married, she was a member of the well known Pease family of Darlington. There is a life sized statue of one of the Pease family in the centre of Darlington. There was another branch of Peases who lived in Bristol.

My Grandmother who accompanied my mother to Staithes was called Lucy Anne Pease and she had a sister called Katherine Aldam Pease who became Enid's close companion after Lucy had a stroke whilst lifting a bookcase to free their dog 'Leo'. Lucy's difficulties due to semi-paralysis are quite apparent when reading the diary. Katherine later married Sir Thomas Hanbury, who created a splendid botanical garden and villa in Italy, assisted by sixty botanical experts. Enid used to frequently stay with her Aunt in Italy. Some years ago, this famous estate 'La Mortola' was the subject of a BBC documentary.

Whilst growing up I often admired a delightful large oil painting we had of the two sweet innocent young girls sitting in a lovely garden. The older sister Lucy was painted in a forget-me-not blue silken dress with pumps also in satin to match. Katherine was dressed similarly in white. Lucy was teaching Katherine to read as they were sitting outside in the garden with beech trees as a background.

Lucy Ann Pease Robinson
with Leo ~ circa 1897

I have unearthed a wide selection of interesting essays in several books inspired by Enid, some of which have beautiful sketches and watercolours in them. Enid wrote about Aunt Katherine, and detailed descriptions of staying near Bristol in a beautiful mansion called 'Cote Bank' giving accounts of the various aunts and uncles and their lifestyles in the 1900s. I think the last days of Katherine after Sir Thomas Hanbury's death, was that she left Italy, and came to stay with her relations Daniel and Sylvia Hanbury at 'Castle Malwood' near Southampton. James Hart tells me the diary was discovered for sale close to Southampton, so it remains a strong possibility this diary could have been in safe keeping with Enid's Aunt Katherine who died in 1920.

All I can say is that my mother was very gifted, with numerous talents. She was a brilliant freelance artist and sketched what came naturally. She was very well read and we used to tease her and call her "the family dictionary". In her youth there was no such thing as colour photography or quick snapping in a flash, but she had a retentive memory and fully absorbed nature happening all around her. She had the ability to catch scenes, when she sat quietly in thought and later recalled them in sketches and verse. Some of the sketches were fantastic, often expressed with wit and very amusing. Even in later life after she became an amputee, she felt no pity, and joked that it was such a shame as she always thought she had a lovely pair of ankles! My husband and I always looked forward to her coming to stay, when she would often sit in the garden in her wheel chair, drinking in the beauty of nature and writing her lovely poetry.

My mother leaves a bounty of beauty for others to share and appreciate.

To the readers I express all my good wishes towards their enjoyment of her gifts.

From her daughter
Honor Theresa Pullen

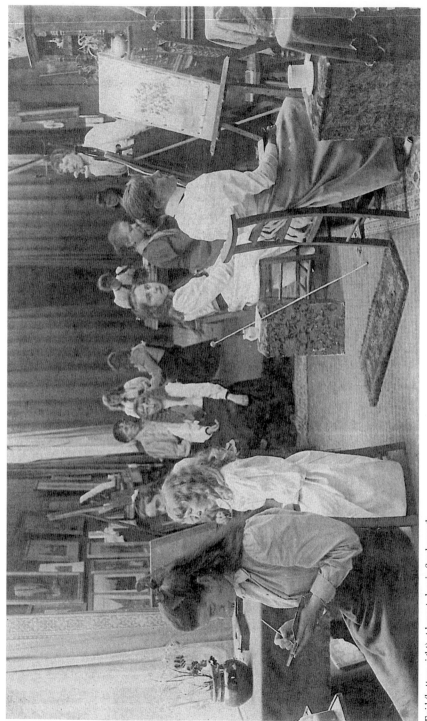

Enid (bottom right) at her art class in Scarborough.

Introduction by James Hart

May I first of all say a huge thank you to Honor for her informative introduction to the diary of her late mother and also for granting permission to posthumously publish the entire contents.

After discovering the diary for sale at auction and purchasing it unseen, then subsequently realising the quality and historical significance of Enid's skillfully written work, the quest was on to trace Enid's living descendants, without whose permission this diary couldn't be published. I would like to thank Lynn Green of Sedgefield for her kind assistance researching Enid's lineage and Chris Lloyd of the Darlington Northern Echo for the article he ran, which ultimately led me to Honor in the Lake District. It was a privilege to meet Honor, read the diary together and talk to her at length. She kindly showed me many photographs (some published here) and more of her mother's other artwork and writing.

At our meeting, we could only speculate about what had become of the diary since it was first written in 1901. We knew it was sourced from a West Sussex auction room, not far from the address where Enid was living in 1901. Her father, Robert Robinson, was a civil engineer and at this time was working on a contract and living with his family away from their home town of Darlington at Leeson Manor, Langton Matravers, near Swanage. Did Enid hide the diary in Leeson Manor? Alternatively, there is the Southampton connection mentioned by Honor, but if anyone reading this book can shed any light, especially the last custodian, we would be very interested to hear from them via our website. Furthermore, the fact that this diary was written in 1901 during Enid's annual pilgrimage to Staithes, raises the exciting possibility that there are other Staithes journals prior to 1901 out there waiting to be discovered. Does anyone recall seeing any other material?

Why 'Secret Diary'?

After writing the diary, Enid had perhaps felt some embarrassment or unease about its contents. Fortunately, she couldn't bring herself to destroy the diary, so proceeded to hide all the location names and some of the characters by methodically inking out all but the first letter in most instances of those words, making it extremely difficult for any other reader to decipher the diary. However, through the wonders of modern technology, and shining a small LED torch through the back of each page, it was possible to reveal the darker double ink impression, thus revealing the secret hidden words. I hope Enid will forgive me for this!

Again, we can only speculate as to the reason for this deliberate blotting out, but Enid was a well protected only child and there is a strong possibility that she feared her father would read the diary and reprimand her. It is hinted within the text that her sojourns in Staithes and her fraternising with the free spirited artists was frowned upon by him, despite being accompanied by her mother.

In presenting this diary to you, I have included some facsimile pages showing Enid's beautiful writing, but for purposes of reproduction and ease of reading, conceded it was not practical or cost effective to produce a full facsimile and typed text in the one book. However, in order for you to know which words were partially deleted, the hidden letters are printed in a lighter grey shade. Except for revealing the hidden words, integrity of the diary has been maintained by ensuring that all words and punctuation remain as written.

My fascination with Staithes' history was fired by my late father, Kenneth, and I would like to dedicate this book to his memory. Without use of the internet, he amassed a good collection of books, articles and turn of the century postcards from the village. These photographic postcards along with the paintings by late 19th and early 20th century Staithes artists are the only visual records from a time shortly before the general use of ciné film and recording of sound. It has long frustrated me that there are no known first hand immediately written accounts of life in Staithes, but always believed that something must exist out there, and it was only a matter of time before something like this was found. To the best of my knowledge, the only comparable prior work is Dame Laura Knight's autobiographical 'Oil Paint and Grease Paint', which has a few chapters describing in detail her times in Staithes. It is fascinating to compare Laura Knight's version of Dick Longster's drowning with the possibly more naïve account of the same event given by Miss Robinson, unless her reference to 'spiritual things' bears a double entendre! Enid Lucy Pease Robinson was exactly four years and two days Laura Knight's junior:

Oil Paint and Grease Paint – First Volume
Chapter VII – Aud Jarge.

Of all the religious people in Staithes he (George Longster) was the most fervent. He knew the bible by heart. The tragedy in his life was that his younger brother was a drunkard.

One wild night, when the tide was running high, the brother left the 'Cod and Lobster' at closing time and was never seen again. "He must a' missed his way at t'corner and gone int' sea." The railed bulwark by the stone slipway where the 'Cod and Lobster' stood was dangerous, even in the daytime. When there was a "wind" and high tide running no one could pass because of the tons of water coming over; they had to squeeze through Dog Lope. We had seen part of the old 'Cod and Lobster' washed down soon after we got there, before they built a bulwark to protect the new one.

No one had seen the brother after he went staggering out into the darkness; he just disappeared. The next day his body was washed up on the beach. When it was being carried up, "Aud Jarge" from his window saw and came out of his house to meet it. He told the men to put the corpse down on the quay just where they were. There and then, he delivered an impassioned speech while standing over it. After praying to God to forgive his brother, he turned to the crowd, exhorting them to repent of their evil before it was too late.

"My pore brither has died in sin! All ye who sin take heed, lest like him ye are caught unawares and go down to the bottomless pits of Hell, into the fires that are never quenched."

For those readers who are unfamiliar with Staithes and the rugged North Yorkshire coast, you may first wish to read the brief introduction at the back of this book. Many thanks to Reg Firth, the curator and owner of Staithes museum, for his help and advice in this regard. It was through my conversations with Reg that he pinpointed one of the locations where Enid would sit and relax with her mother and consequently the image chosen for the front cover of this book:

'The Lookout' by Robert Jobling. Thanks also to Ian Walker of Walker Galleries, Harrogate, for obtaining an image of the original painting which passed through his hands some years ago. Laura Knight describes 'the lookout' beautifully:

Oil Paint and Grease Paint – First Volume
Chapter VI – White Water.

"There were two posts set on this ledge, on which lamps were hung at night. When the boats came home in the dark, they had only to keep them in sight one above the other, as they rowed in a safe channel, clear of the sunken reefs on either side. There was romance in those lights that guided the men home..."

Laura Knight wrote about the annual exhibitions of paintings which the artists held in Staithes, but frustratingly, she does not go so far as giving dates. Perhaps one of the most exciting pieces of information contained herein is Enid's account of the inaugural Staithes Art Club exhibition, opened on Monday 26th August 1901. Art historians have long sought documentary evidence of this first exhibition, only presumed to have been held in 1901, given that the earliest extant records relate to the second exhibition held in August 1902. We are indebted to Enid for this wonderful, and thus far, unique historic passage.

Before I leave the diary with you, I give thanks to my wife Sharon, for her patience in taking responsibility for more than her fair share of our domestic workload over the past year or so, becoming somewhat, something of a 'Staithes widow'. However, she contends that was already the case!

I sincerely hope you enjoy reading Miss Enid Lucy Pease Robinson's diary.

James Hart, January 2010

Enid . L . Pease Robinson
Leeson Manor,
Langton Matravers,
Near Swanage
Dorset.

STAITHES
1901

August 7th (Wednesday) 1901

We left Darlington by the 2 o'clock train, and arrived at Staithes at 4.20, after an uneventful journey. We had Mr Harding as far as Saltburn where he was going to attend a meeting, and after that, we had the carriage to ourselves, for which we were rather glad. I was at any rate, for I was feeling quite sick the whole way, with rushing off so soon after lunch. Trains always make me feel sick too. Arrived at Staithes, we went straight down to Mrs Brown's, whose rooms we have taken this year, and had tea, as we were really famished. No sign of D, so we asked Mrs Brown if he had come and she said he had not, but that nearly all the other visitors who were here last year had come again this year. What do I care for them, if the one person I came to see is not here! The place is simply overrun with women and children! I thought Staithes would always be free from the latter, at all events, as it is dangerous for them with the cliffs and tides etc. After tea, I could not bear being in the house, – I felt choked, so mother and I went out to buy some tea at Featherstone's and to post a post card to Father to say that we had arrived safely, and we then went on to the quay, and saw Mrs Ward, who has lost her daughter Margaret, poor thing (the one who was dying of consumption when we were last here) since we were at Staithes last year. After speaking to her for about 10 minutes, we went on to speak to Mrs Thompson's party, who were all sitting outside the door of their cottage, knitting, and waiting until it was time for the boats to go off. Everybody seems either ill or dying; it is dreadful – so depressing!

Poor old Dick (Longster) is dead! He was coming home, it is supposed, one dark night, when he stumbled, and fell over the Staith! Nothing was known of all this until his familiar figure was missed next day, and the daughter came running in to ask Mrs Thompson if she had seen anything of him, as he had not been along to see her (his daughter) as usual, and she could not find him in his own cottage. Mrs Thompson went with her to look again, and they found that the bed had never been slept in. Then they raised the alarm, and his body was subsequently, discovered out on the rocks, washed out to sea! Poor old Dick, I am sorry. He was such a dear, true, good old man, and he was so fond of Mother and me, – "t'laady an' t' darter", as he called us. He was a firm believer in spiritual things, so I hope he has gone to that heaven on which his thoughts so constantly dwelt.

Then poor Mrs Thompson has lost her old mother, though she said quite cheerfully, "Mi Mother's dead yer knaw" – still, I'm sure she feels it much more than she shows. She is of a cheery, hopeful temperament which nothing apparently, can subdue, – and well for her and for the poor in general (for they all possess it in a greater or less degree) that it is so, or the cruel troubles which they have to bear would prove quite insupportable.

Mrs Thompson introduced us to Mrs Barrett, – who is a funny plebeian old party; shouldn't suppose her husband finds much joy in her, though he is not of very prepossessing appearance.

I observed Mr Mayor and Mr Friedenson on the Staith; they both looked hard at me. Then Misses Jobling (all three) also came along, and we bowed to them, and they to us. I saw their father going down to paint, over the Beck, but I don't think he saw me as I was up in our sitting room window.

Mrs Thompson says that Mr Rigg's dear old mother has been very ill and in consequence, he has not been over in Staithes for sometime now. Her son's wife died, leaving three little children, so the dear little Grannie went over to Bradford (I suppose) to try and comfort the poor father, and bring the little ones back with her, for a change. The fuss and worry, however, proved too much for her, and she fell ill, and has been ill all the summer, poor dear little old lady.

Mr Bagshawe is engaged to be married in three weeks time to a Miss Turnbull, the only daughter of a ship owner at Whitby, and has been casting about for a house in Staithes, which should be to let, unfurnished, for the summer.

-owner at Whitby, and he has been casting about for a house on ███, which should be to let, unfurnished, for the summer.

Miss Good is married, and is already ᴵⁿ ᴾᵃʳⁱˢ on her honeymoon tour.

The Aunt of The Johnson girls, who was here one year, (1897) is dead, poor Thing, but they did not go into black for her.

The second Ward Baby (a boy, James) has developed the same sores on his hands as his sister Meggie had a year or two ago. The doctor says it is constitutional, like this poor mother's consumption and D, says Mrs Porritt, is

Miss Good is married and is already in Paris on her honeymoon tour.

The Aunt of the Johnson girls, who was here one year (1897) is dead, poor thing, but they did not go into black for her.

The second Ward baby (a boy, James) has developed the same sores on his hands as his sister Meggie had a year or two ago. The doctor says it is constitutional, like his poor mother's consumption, and D, says Mrs Porritt is at Scarborough – "too ill to go away", or as she put it, "E's in the hen-joy-ment of very poor ealth, por young mahn!" That was all; but what a world it meant to me! All the difference between heaven upon earth and the exact opposite! Oh dear, <u>why</u> is life made up of contrarieties?

I saw that ugly girl, "Ethel", (I am sure it was she). I suppose she will miss him too! How I dislike her, and yet, I can't help feeling rather sorry for her, for her passion is quite hopeless, as he alludes to her, somewhat contemptuously as "that other girl"! How all the world is angling for something that they can't get!

After speaking to Mrs Ward again, Mother and I went for a walk on the other side of the beck, to look up old Joe Verrill, but found him out, and, as Mr Jobling was painting just opposite, we went up and spoke to him, and he said that Mrs Jobling had heard we were coming, and had asked him to look out for us! How people do know all one's plans here! However it is rather pleasant, in a way, to be so welcomed back. After this we went for a walk up the Cliff Road, but as I was longing to cry the whole time, I got mother at last to agree to our returning, on the plea of it growing too dark and chilly, – though the sky was lovely, – a delicate pale silver grey, with a darker line for the sea, on the horizon, and beautiful gleaming light on the softly rippling water far below. Mr Bagshawe evidently thought it was lovely too, for he was gazing out to sea and up at the gathering masses of fleecy grey clouds, with a very solemn expression, quite unlike his usual merry mischievous self. He has changed much during the past year, it must be his impending marriage. How tired I feel, – and poor mother too! I am going to bed now to have a good cry.

I cried half the night, and woke in very low spirits, but felt better as the day wore on, and the blessed sunshine broke through the black threatening clouds overhead. Mother and I read on the quay and shore all day, and in the evening, mother actually managed to get as far as Hinderwell! – a great achievement for her. We got in rather late, though. Kept hoping that D might come all day, but he never turned up. Mrs Brown, our landlady, a sweet, sad-faced woman has been telling us some very naughty tales that are current in the village concerning that beast Mayor and even poor little "Friedie". She says the fisher-boys go and watch their proceedings in their stocking feet!! Poor little "Friedie" looks so very harmless and good-natured, and if he would not do an unkind turn to anybody, but he said to someone here that he is too poor to marry, and if he can barely support himself, how is he going to support a wife? I think rich or well-off self-righteous people are too hard on those who are too poor (and too healthy!) to be moral – and poor little F looks the picture of health! He does look diminutive by all the other artists, except "Riggie" though!

There is such a handsome man here, – Mr Richardson – who looks exactly like a foreigner, – with hair and moustache as black as ink, and a swarthy complexion, and a nice gentlemanly, easy walk. He was here last year, but he seems to have improved wonderfully in appearance from what I remember him to have been. I suppose it is not a case of mistaken identity. He is just like a dark edition of the "B.W." – quite a marvel of masculine beauty! What a pity he isn't fair instead!

I have been asking Mrs Brown about him, and she says he is not Mr Richardson, but a Mr Swinstead, who, with his wife, – a quiet, pale fairish plump woman, always dressed in drab, and two little boys in red jerseys, and their nurse, and are lodging at Mrs Laverick's further up the street. They were here last year, so I have seen him before, but I had not known that the woman and children belonged to him, as I have never yet seen either of them together!, he goes off painting by himself, it appears, and leaves them to their own devices! His name and address are:– F H Swinstead, Ivy Bank, Crouch End Hill, London, N.

F.H.S. ▪

Ivy Bank
Crouch End Hill
London N.

Another lovely morning with occasional cloudy glooms. I keep hoping against hope that D may yet turn up, but I have fits of great depression about him. I have even begun to wonder whether he <u>drinks</u>, though it is a suspicion which I should not dream of mentioning to a single soul, – not even mother! She <u>has</u> been good! So sweet and sympathetic! I don't really know what I should do without her, though at times she depresses me still more by taking the most gloomy view possible, whilst at others, she takes the brightest views, and when she does not <u>make a palpable effort</u> in that direction, she cheers me wonderfully.

I keep watching at the window for him every day, and every time there is a train, and some people descend the hill from the station, I rush to the window hoping to see the familiar figure and the bright red hair (just fancy! I used to think red hair absolutely hideous, once upon a time, before I knew <u>him</u>! But then I had never seen a <u>handsome</u>, or even, tolerably good-looking man with red hair, so it was not much wonder!) – But he never comes, and I go back and choke down my dinner, and than let off my feelings alone upstairs, in my room! There is nothing to distract my thoughts either and mother can't go for a quick walk, so I grow awfully morbid. I feel as if we had been here three weeks already, instead of three days, –

"We should count time by heart-throbs,
He most lives, who thinks most, feels the most," etc.

I really think, if D does not come soon, that I shall send for Elsie to cheer me up, dear child, she is a wonderful person to fly to when one is in trouble.

There are two extraordinary specimens of humanity here who are universally known by their Christian names of 'Charlie' and 'Sydney'. I have not seen such sketches for a long time! They come from Australia, their fathers both having large ranches there, – and they are going for a tour all round the coast of England, I hear. They have taken the old dilapidated cottage next to old Joe Verrill's, where the Johnsons' studio used to be, and have christened it "<u>WHAREPUNI</u>"

"Sydney"

(the name is printed in large ornamental reddish – brown letters on a card about one and a half feet long across the top of the door). They have furnished it with two hammocks, in which they sleep, a cooking stove, on which they do all their own cooking, a pair of chairs, a plain deal table, and, I conclude, a bath-tub, (but this they may borrow from neighbours!) since they do their own washing, <u>WHEN</u> <u>IT</u> <u>IS</u> <u>DONE</u>!, they wear no collars, nor any unnecessary clothes (especially not linen ones) and are about as unkempt a pair as one could find this side of the workhouse! – about like the casuals who turn in there for a night, except that casuals don't wear white hats, which (S)ydney and (C)harlie do. Sydney's name is Thompson (for I got Mrs Brown to ask everybody until she did find out, eventually, what it was!) – and Charlie's name is Sanderson.

"Charlie"

A really glorious morning! My hopes rose high this morning, and I almost expected that D. would come, but the day wore on, and train-load after train-load came and went, and still no D! I am afraid I must give up hoping for him, now, – though he might come on Monday, – but oh, it is hard! I thought at last I was going to have a few weeks of unalloyed happiness, after all I went through last winter, – but no! it appears it is not to be. I wonder if D worries about me even half as much as I worry about him? But I can not and do not expect that; men never do. They never love to the extent that women do, when once their heart is fixed on one man, and one only. Besides, it would be hatefully selfish of me to wish him to worry; but should like to know that he thought of me sometimes – a little bit every day, for I think of him every day and all day long, and however short my prayers may be, they always include him, with father and mother. I had a kind of presentiment, about three days before we came here, that I should not see him, and do what I would, I could not shake this horrid cold feeling off; I even began to wonder, in a curious impersonal sort of way, if I could possibly have given up loving him, and I began to see all his worst points (such as they are) – and I felt hopelessly unsettled and wretched in my mind all the time before we started, though I began to shake it off, and to look forward to seeing him, when I was in the train. I felt quite sick with disappointment when Mrs Brown said he was not here, and I still feel as if there were a great lump of lead at the bottom of my throat!

About 4 o'clock in the afternoon, after a broiling morning, a heavy thunder storm broke over here. I went to Mrs Thompson's cottage, as soon as I saw it coming on, as one can see the lightening there so beautifully – I stood in the door, and watched it playing round Cowbar Nab, and out at sea – it was sublimely beautiful, and so near too. The thunder was like the explosions of a powder magazine just overhead, but we were quite safe in Mrs Thompson's low cottage, and I could watch, to my full satisfaction how the great ribbons of pink and blue lightening shot across the cliffs, and how the pelting rain came down almost in bucketfuls, ploughing up the sea and covering it with a steaming white and grey mist, and washing the Staith as clean as if it had been mopped with soap-and-water. Then a strong wind sprang up, all of a sudden, and blew as if it would blow the whole of Staithes into the sea. The sea itself was sent swurging all ways at once, for the currents converged, and then flew apart like "cannoned" billiard-balls. It was a grand sight. I grew rather anxious about mother, though, for I thought she would be worrying about me, though I was perfectly safe where I was, – so, as soon as the rain would permit, I ran along back to the Bank, and found mother sitting talking to Mrs Brown and the children, and watching the storm. After I got in, it came on badly again, and the sky looked grand, – a deep, coppery red on the horizon, and a blue-black overhead. The lightning too was most vivid. I stood in the porch and watched it, in spite of mother's repeated warnings, as I felt absolutely stifled inside, the air was so close. It was too wet to go for a walk after tea, so we stayed in, and wrote, read etc, to try and drown our thoughts.

August 11th (Sunday) 1901

This morning, as there is no church here, I thought I would go hear Miss Featherstone's darling, the Rev J.O.Warburton, preach his last sermon, at the Wesleyan Chapel (!!) before he is moved on in the course of the circuit. He is the young man whom Miss F introduced to Betty Davis, and who caused B such secret amusement by taking her hand, holding it for a long time, meanwhile gazing with a look of rapt attention and admiration into Betty's pretty face, and saying in a sentimental voice, "and are you VERY well?" – He certainly amused me extremely, this morning! I have never been to a Wesleyan Methodist Chapel except once before, (when I was about 7 years old, and father and mother wanted to hear some rather celebrated preacher – I forget his name, – so they went to the Bondgate Wesleyan Chapel instead of the church or meeting that morning) – so I was both amused and interested in all I saw and heard. I thought I was dreadfully late and imagined by the comparative silence that they must be having a prayer, so I stood undecided outside the door, until a very ugly old fisherman with a rough, cheerful face, and his little gooseberry-eyed grandson came clumping and trotting up the stone flagged passage from the street.

"I don't know, – could you tell me which is the right door, please?" I said, feeling very shy and uncomfortable – the old man grinned amicably, and said cheerfully, "ah's gaun in! yer can foller me!" – so I did. When we got inside, he said in a whisper that could have been heard all over the building, in spite of all the whispering and talking that was going on all the time, "Yer can sit in MAH pew if yer laikes!!" as if he were a king granting a dukedom! So I thankfully accepted this immense favour, as I felt very shy and uncomfortable since the whole congregation had turned its eyes upon poor unfortunate me, and all the female portion were whispering remarks about my clothes, (I wore my black velvet picture hat, black gauze ruffle, white openwork blouse, and sea green skirt, with a string of pink Venetian beads, – my last birthday present from Rhoda Wolley). Then the young person at the organ (I dignify it with that name, though it had only about 7 small pipes) commenced to play "see the conquering hero comes", and in walked the Rev: J.O.Warburton, with his top hat on. He bobbed behind the sort of ticket-office erection of pitch-pine, with a stair-railing round it, and an office table of the same wood in front, in the drawer of which the square red hymn books are kept, – and after about 3 seconds, suddenly bobbed up above the top of the ticket-office, minus his top hat. He then sat down on the right hand side of the balcony at the top, put on a pious expression, and began to meditate until the last strains of "see the conquering hero comes", had died away (or was it "Toll for the Brave, – the Brave that are no more?" – anyway it was Handel's "March in Scipio"). This finished, up jumped Mr Warburton, and said in a startlingly sudden voice, as if he had only just awakened to his responsibilities "Let us worship God!" Then came a hymn, and Mr Featherstone creaked up to the office table, drew out the drawer in a very matter of fact way, took out a hymn book, creaked down the isle again, with a beaming smile and handed it to me!

After the hymn came a long prayer, in which Mr Warburton thanked God that we do not hallways see thy photograph in the ragin' storm, – the rollin' thunder, and the vivid lightnin'; we sometimes see thy photograph in the calm sea, and the bright sunshine, an' the bee-ootiful blue sky, has we do this mornin'!' – and an old fisherman who sat in the pew in front of my old fisherman, said "Aa - MEN!" In a very loud voice!!!

Then followed other hymns and prayers, the last prayer being modelled on that contained in the church-service for "all those who are in any way afflicted in mind, body or estate"; this one was really very nice and unexceptionable, excepting for Mr Warburton's pronunciations instead of praying as we do for "Jews, Turks and Infidels", he prayed for "The Roman Catholics, the Church of England and EVEN the Salvation Harmy!" How narrow all religious bodies are! It is quite painful to see each sect thinking that it is only right, and that it only will be saved, whilst all the other will go to eternal damnation, unless they be carefully prayed for by the one elect body, which then feels very self-righteous for having prayed for its enemies! After all this, Mr Warburton, raising his voice, said, "I will now proceed dear bretheren, to give you a short <u>HEX</u>–<u>PO</u>–<u>SITION</u> on the verse which you will find if you open your bibles at …….." (great rustling of leaves). During the course of the "Hex-<u>PO</u>-sition", Mr Warburton mentioned that the "Hapos<u>t</u>les were not <u>er</u>-<u>U</u>-<u>dite</u> men", and that something or other was not "faysuble!" (feasible). But his closing remarks were really irresistibly funny! He said "Now, mhay deeur bretheren, I can not claws (by the way, he said that all Jesus' "<u>claws</u>" were "transfigured along with his face!!") without tellin' you hov won little hincident. I think the thing that'as struck me most of all I ever 'eard, was a true story of a <u>CON</u>-verted swape (sweep) oo lived on the town I was born in. Now this swape, – William Tilly was 'is name. – used to lead a very bad, vicious laife; e was <u>halways</u> drunk, and if <u>any</u>body was ever 'ad up for wife–beatin', it was <u>halways</u> this drunken swape. But a few years agaw, 'e went to —— chapel, and under the Rev:——— 'e got soundly <u>CON</u>-verted. Well 'e was very 'appy in 'is new–found love, and 'e wanted to witness for Jesus, like a true Christian, – wanted everybody to naw about Jesus, and to luv 'im, as 'e did. Well, there were some mills in the town, and for some weeks hevery year they are laid idle, while the directors are stock–takin'!, and this year they sent for the poor swape to clean the flaws!, (at first I thought he meant "floors", though I thought a char-woman would have been a more suitable person to undertake <u>that</u> job than even a <u>CON</u>-verted chimney-sweep! Finally, however, I discovered that by "flaws", Mr Warburton intended to convey to the congregation the word "<u>flues</u>") Well, the directors were talkin' in one of the rooms an' they didn't knaw that the poor swape was down the flaw, so they were a good deal <u>SUR</u>-prised when they 'eard a sort of scratchin' sound down the flaw, so one of them put 'is 'ead in at the 'ole, and called down into the flaw "<u>OO's</u> <u>there</u>?" – and the annser came up from the depths of that black, dirty, flaw, —— "<u>WILLIAM TILLY AN' THE LORD JESUS CHRIST</u>"" (Imagine the astonishment of the poor director! Enid.L.P.R).

"Now, mhay dear bretheren, it isn't <u>all</u> of us that could take the Lord Jesus Christ down into a flaw with us, – <u>is</u> it? – and I think I never 'eard of a more glorious triumph of Methodism than that poor swape's brave witnessin' of Jesus!".

I told all this to mother when I got home, and she was much amused – but of course I don't wish to laugh at all of it, or I should be as narrow as the Methodists themselves, – but, truly, this sort of thing presents infinite and irresistible humour to an ordinarily well-educated mind, though it is all very well for the working-classes, who are not possessed of a keen sense of humour, and who take it all in deadly earnest, and even say "Aa - MEN!" like the dear old fisherman, – it is just like a play at religion, – a sort of parody – all this chapelism, and there is nothing whatever dignified about it, like there is about our beautiful Church of England. Never did I realise to the full the grandeur and beauty of the Church as opposed to dissent than I did this morning! I couldn't be a chapelite now, for anything!

In the afternoon we sat and read on the quay and the "lookout" (the higher one) until it began to rain, and we then came in until church-time at 5. (The service here has to be held at 5 o'clock, as Mr Moore has a service at Hinderwell Church at 6.30, and as there is no curate, it is all he can do to fit it all in, though Mr Crompton is coming back, I am glad to say. Poor Mr Moore looks quite worn-out and overdone).

I felt very dismal about D – all this evening.

August 12th (Monday) 1901

This morning, as we were sitting at breakfast, I saw a familiar little figure descending the hill from the station. It was dear little "Riggie", and I flew to the window to watch him go past, but as he evidently did not know where we were lodging, he did not look up at all, but just went straight on down towards the quay. I scuttled through my breakfast, and rushed upstairs to put on my pretty hat with the pink roses in it, and my string of pink Venetian beads, and to change my somewhat soiled pale-blue tie for a clean white lace one – I then seized my book, "Wisdom and Destiny", and my work (the old peacock on a blue linen ground! it gets on at about the rate of ½ an inch per week!) and feeling horribly nervous and shaky, went out on to the quay, and pretended to be entirely unaware of R's existence until I got opposite to him. He, likewise, having watched me furtively as I came on to the quay, pretended to be extraordinarily interested in the sea, and not to be in the least aware of my presence, until I got up to him, when he turned around suddenly and came forward, trying to control his features, for he was quite as nervous and shy as I was, dear little man! He had been talking to "Friedie" and the youth like Mr "Mason", with the brown velvet cap, just before, and they both turned round, and stared rather rudely. He gave my hand a great hearty grip, and said, "Well, Miss Robinson, I am pleased to see you back at Staithes again!" and I certainly never saw anybody look more pleased over anything! Then I said, "Thank you very much! Yes, it's nice to be back again in our old haunts. I was so sorry to hear how ill your mother had been; I hope she's better now?" – "Thank you, yes, she's mending nicely, I think, but she's not downstairs yet – Oh, she's had a very bad time, and the doctors never thought she would pull through, you know – congestion of the lungs!" – "Oh, I didn't know it was as bad as that! I am sorry! – and what an anxious time you must have had too!" – "Oh, yes, I've had a lot of worry – I haven't been doing any painting, much lately, you know, with mother so ill, I sat up with her, night and day, and I had to send for all my brothers and sisters once, because we thought she wouldn't pull through! Oh, it was an awful time!", I hardly knew what to say, I felt so sorry for the dear little true hearted man! After a few moments' silence, he said very shyly, but very ardently, "Miss Robinson, I DO WISH that you and Mrs Robinson would come over some evening, and, – we might have a little music?" (– this rather timidly) Here was a fix! What was I to say! I mumbled something about its being "very kind" etc, etc – and then once more he pleaded, "DO!" Feeling myself driven to bay, I said that I was afraid that mother couldn't walk so far, as she so soon got tired. "But you could come by train couldn't you?" he said half reproachfully, half hopefully! Now I was hopelessly cornered, so thanked him again, and said I would ask mother. I simply couldn't resist those dog-like eyes! Then I said I was going to settle down outside Mrs Thompson's, and he said "good-morning". It appears however, that he met mother in the High Street and asked her, personally about our going there and she didn't see any way out of it, so she at last consented to go when his mother should be better. I hope the whole village won't get to know about it, and gossip, or couple our names together, like they do about "Mayor" and "Friedie", and the ugly girl with the flappy hat! "Riggie" didn't go, however; he came back and talked to Mrs Thompson near us, and then went up the back passage to see old Mr Thompson, and then came back and talked to us again, and seemed as if he couldn't tear himself away, dear little soul. Meanwhile, black clouds were gathering overhead, and before we knew where we were, a severe thunder-storm was upon us! We scrambled all our things together, and R. said he was going to catch the 1.37 train to Hinderwell, but the storm came on so badly, that mother asked him to come up and shelter in our rooms, which he gratefully accepted. I got in first, as I had to run, because the rain would have spoilt my clothes if I had not, and I left mother, who had at least a parasol, behind.

I rushed up to change my hat, and get an umbrella and was going out to meet mother with it, when I heard her calling up the stairs, "Enid! Mr Rigg's coming in to shelter with us!" At that moment, Riggie and I nearly collided on the landing, as he had come up before mother, and I very nearly knocked a bracket with a little lamp on it, down, in my confusion! He smiled very kindly, and said, "take care!", then we came in and I asked him to sit down. I went and stood by the window, and watched the lightening playing over the housetops, "That's not a very safe position, is it, Miss Robinson?" he said – "Oh, I don't know!" I said laughing nervously – "I love watching the lightning!" – "Why, you seem to have no fear whatever, Miss Robinson!" he said, "no!" I answered, laughing, "I don't think I am afraid of most things!" Then I called to him to come and look at a great flock of sea-birds wheeling overhead, and then mother came in, and asked me where the Leeson House photographs were. I fished them out, and we spent a very happy half-hour looking at them, and then he said he would not detain us from our lunch any longer, so he got up, and smilingly backed out of the room, when mother showed him the photographs which Sylvia took of me at Leeson, and I said I thought the "elegant" one in the daisy-field was flattered, he looked very serious, and said, in a tone which sounded like "How can you say such a thing?" – "It isn't flattered at all, Miss Robinson! Not one bit!" Poor little Riggie! It is quite evident from the look in his eyes, what is going on in his dear, true, faithful little heart! I am dreadfully sorry, for his sake, that it is so! But I don't see how I can prevent it, for if I were suddenly to turn unkind to him now, he would not understand that it was for his own good, any more than my dear faithful Leo would, if I were to take a poisoned bone from him, or whip him away from a spring-trap.

I felt quite cheered up with seeing poor little Riggie, and, in the evening, mother and I had the most cheerful walk we have had since we came, though we did not get further than the Lane End Houses. Before this, our walks have closely resembled funeral processions, or the constitutional of those religious orders, who, are forbidden by their vows even to speak.

A dullish morning, with occasional gleams of sunshine. I awoke in a more hopeful frame of mind than I have been in ever since we came, – all because of poor little Riggie! – Though I still feel very sad about my dear D, and all that he must be suffering. I sat on the "Honeymooners' Rock" and sewed and read by turns. In the afternoon, as it came out beautifully fine, I told mother that I couldn't be stewed up in Staithes any longer, and that I was going for a walk somewhere by myself, as she could neither walk fast nor far enough to give me even a tolerable amount of exercise. She demurred at first, and said it wasn't suitable, but at last she said that she would go by train to Hinderwell and I could walk there. So I had a delightful quick walk out to Hinderwell and as far as the Runswick Bay Hotel, but a fearful scurry back in time to meet mother, for they told me at the hotel that it was 10 minutes past four, and the train came in at 4.13. I got there just in time to see it puffing out of the station, so I suppose it must have been a little late. Mother was walking about, waiting for me, so after getting a drink of water at the station, (for I was so horribly thirsty with walking so fast in all the heat) we walked on to Runswick, – to the top of the bank, – and sat on the seat overlooking the lovely bay, which lay blue and calm in the evening sunlight, with the little gaily painted fishing boats gently rising and falling with each rippling wave, far below. Crowds of children were on the sands, and the sound of the waves breaking on the beach came to us only as a faint murmur. Everything seemed steeped in peace; if only D had been there, it would have been perfect, and there would have been nothing left to wish for!

"We look before and after,
And pine for what I not:
Our sincerest laughter
With some pain is fraught
Our sweetest songs are those
That tell of saddest thought"

True O'Shelley! – D's favourite poet!

about, waiting for me, so
after getting a drink of
water at the station, (for
I was so horribly thirsty
with walking so fast
in all the heat) we walked
on to R████████ — to the
top of the bank, — and
sat on the seat overlooking
the lovely bay, which lay blue and
calm in the evening sunlight,
with the little gaily painted
fishing boats gently rising
and falling with each
rippling wave, far below.
Crowds of children were
on the sands, and the
sound of the waves breaking
on the beach came to us
only as a faint murmur.
Everything seemed steeped
in peace; if only I had been

37

We sat there, and watched the people climbing the steep bank to go back to their "teas" at Hinderwell like cows returning to the byre at milking–time. Amongst them, to my great surprise, I saw 'Sydney' and 'Charlie', with a large family–party!! First, came Sydney, carrying a small child in a very uncomfortable position, with one arm over his shoulder, held by his left hand, and both its legs dangling behind, whilst it sat on his right hand. It evidently, did not relish this position, for it was howling lustily! Then came 'Charlie', with a small boy in leather leggings, then the father of the family, then a queer little deformed hunchback, probably the uncle, and then the mother with another little girl. They all wended their way towards the station, and came on to Staithes – They are here now, – quite ordinary–looking mortals – when one of them (a fat, stubby, red–faced one) suddenly rushed up with great joy to mother, and exclaimed "Oh, Mrs Robinson, how do you do!" After a short conversation on the beauty of the place and the evening, etc. and after she had said that they came over for the day every year, she took her departure, and I immediately turned to mother and gasped "who on earth is that?" mother laughed, and said she did not know her name, but that she was a cousin of Miss Mellanby's, who used to pour out the tea at the Chrysanthemum show, and is now married to a doctor in Saltburn.

After this, it was time for us to go, or we should have missed the train back. We took the shortcut across the fields for two reasons, – one being, that it was shorter than going round by Hinderwell, and the other, that we should not pass Riggie's house by going that way, and so make an awkwardness, perhaps. I wondered rather that he had not been over to Staithes all day, but my doubts were soon dispelled, for the dear little boy turned up all right enough, in the evening. I saw him riding down the hill on his bicycle, and I called out to mother "Oh, there's Riggie, at last" then I rushed for my hat, and walked out, apparently in a great hurry, straight up to Ms Thompson's, only nodding and smiling to R on the way. As usual, he stood gazing out to sea, apparently absorbed in the beauty of the evening, all the time I was coming along the quay, although he had been waiting for me, and knew the precise moment when I was just behind him; as soon as I came opposite to him, he suddenly turned round, as if he had just caught sight of me, and grabbed at his cap, beaming all over. Meanwhile, when I got to Mrs T's, I said, breathlessly, "Oh, Mrs Thompson, did I leave a <u>book</u> here this morning?" (I knew perfectly well that I hadn't – that it was in fact, under my sewing on a chair in the sitting–room, but I had to have some excuse, like <u>D</u> and the ammonites!!) "naw!", said Mrs T laughing, "there's nowt but chairs 'ere!" – and Mary Jane said "'ave yer lost it?" – which I pretended not to hear! I then said that I expected that it was under some other things, and had got hidden, and that I should find it all right in the morning, and bid them "goodnight", and sauntered slowly along the quay, stopping often to gaze at the beautiful soft grey, cloudy sky – at last I got opposite R. again, and he turned round again, and came shyly forward. "Well, Mr Rigg", I said, "are you admiring this lovely sky?, isn't it a beautiful evening?" "Yes, lovely" he answered, and we gazed at the sky for some moments in silence, and made other remarks about it until mother came up – we then had quite a long conversation, until it began to grow quite dark (about 8.30 or 9 o'clock), and then mother said we must go in, and he said, if he might, he would walk so far back with us, so he walked as far as our door, and then bid us good night reluctantly, and walked his bicycle up the hill.

I do not think I mentioned on Monday, that I got old Joe Verrill to help me in a practical joke, which has come off today! When mother and I were sitting over on the other side of the beck, we had been reading out the name of Sydney's and Charlie's house, – "Wharepuni", – and mother suddenly said "what fun it would be to put up a Maori sentence and surprise them! "<u>Ehoä tenaqüa</u>?" ("How do you do?") for instance –" "Oh, <u>wouldn't</u> it!", I said – now, since they had a painted card with the name on. They have painted the space over the top of the door pea–green, and the name in dark-and-pale-green letters in the middle, with a cooking-pot on one side, and an absurd bird with a broken leg (meant for a hen?) running towards it, and a flourish on the other, – thus:–

So I suggested putting "<u>HOROMONA</u> <u>TI</u> <u>ATTUA</u>" (Solomon the GOD, – the name of the handsome New Zealand chief that mother knew) under the idiotic bird!

No sooner said than done! I rushed in for a piece of paper, printed the name on it in bold letters, put a tin-tack through it, and took it down to old Joe I asked him if he would help me in a practical joke? "<u>Ay-hy</u>! That will I!" he chuckled. "What is't?" then I told him, and he said that he thought it would be better if it were <u>pasted</u> up, as it might be blown down by the wind if it were only held by a tack in the middle, and besides, they might ear the hammering, "ah'll get oor aud missus to paaste'n oop, when ah's gaun wi't' booat i't'marnin'!" said old Joe, and this morning he stopped me in the street to say, "ah got oor owd missus ter paaste'n oop. an' by gum, them felleys was naughty aboot'n!" "what did they say?" I asked in fear and trepidation, – "were they <u>angry</u>?" "<u>angry</u>?, whoy, ah shud think they <u>was</u>!, that there Charlie, 'e says to me", "Jaw Verrill, doos thoo knaw owt aboot this 'ere?" "naw!" says ah, "ah deearn't" "yes, thoo doos!" 'e says – "ah tell theh, ah <u>deearn't</u>!" says ah, "<u>ah</u> nivvur putten't theer! Whoy, ah can't neither read nor write, an' ah deearn't knea what it means! What is't ahl aboot?" "whoy", says Charlie, "it means as we've to goa to 'ell!" (what <u>nonsense</u>! Charlie evidently doesn't know his native language, if he thinks <u>that</u>! – unless it has a "double entendre" which mother doesn't know! but then, they would hardly call one of the most handsome of their Maori chiefs, "Go-to-Hell!") "Well, what happened next?" I asked in horror, after explaining to old Joe that it meant nothing of the kind. "Whoy, 'e jus took 'is penknife an' scratched 'en ahl off. 'e said as 'ow it must 'a' bin put on soom tahme. As t' paste wuz sae 'ard!".

By Jove, I hope we shan't be connected with this in any way! Old Joe has promised not to split, and he wouldn't for his own sake either!

August 14ᵗʰ (Wednesday) 1901

A horrid, dismal wet day! No <u>D</u> and no Riggie! Cried nearly all day and half the night too! I got such an awful fright, because I thought I heard old Joe Verrill telling the group of fishermen who always stand just outside our windows, on the angle of the street, at night, all about "<u>Horomona ti atua</u>". My conscience is pricking me awfully; I <u>wish</u> I hadn't done it! Mother says it was her fault for ever suggesting it, but it was mine really, for setting old Joe to do it, for if it had stopped at mother, it would never have been done! And then, I thought the fishermen looked at me as if they had been saying amongst themselves that I had done it. It is true, they always stare hard at me, but I suppose it was an uneasy conscience today – we only went as far as the end of the Staith and back, as the rain was so bad. I have been painting the "High Street, Staithes on a wet day", and have tried to infuse some of <u>D</u>'s style into it, which is, needless to say, very difficult! Oh dear, I do <u>hope</u> old Joe Verrill has not let out our secret!

August 15th (Thursday) 1901

Another horrid wet day! How immeasurably depressing this weather is! Of course, all would be different, if <u>D</u> were here, or even dear, innocent little Riggie. My spirits have been down below zero all day, and I am afraid Charlie and Sydney must have found out about that joke, because they won't look at me now, and they used to stare so hard! Also, the youths from London, who saw it, and said it was what old Joe calls "Mary language", now stare straight before them. Of course, they may all have seen that I take no notice of them, and may therefore think it not worthwhile to stare: I hope it <u>is</u> only that! I will never, <u>never</u> play a practical joke upon total strangers again. I feel it was most unladylike, and I have suffered agonies of "conscience strickenness" since I perpetrated it! Of course, on account of its being so rainy, Riggie did not come tonight, I hope his dear old mother is no worse. I managed to get a sketch done of Cowbar Nab and the rocks at low tide before the rain came on, but as it was not a success, I washed it over with French blue, and called it "evening" (which covers a multitude of sins) and it looks quite unsure work.

A delicious day, after all the hateful rain. I felt quite hopeful again, on the whole, though I don't see that my life can ever be quite the same as it would have been if I had not known <u>D</u>. It is a pity in some ways, as mother often tries to say, only I never will <u>allow</u> her, that such a disturbing influence ever came into my life, – but no! I would rather have all the worry, and have dear <u>D</u> to love and care for than be absolutely heart-whole and free, or have an insipid, quite conventional and proper attachment to someone in our own circle! If I don't marry <u>D</u>, I really don't care <u>whom</u> I marry; all my former sordid ideas about matrimony are returning to me, and if I don't marry <u>him</u>, which, to say the least, is entirely improbable, I shall marry some man who is well-off, and has a handsome, or at any–rate, a <u>good-looking</u> face, and who will let me have pretty much my own way. And I don't care now whether I have any children or not – in fact I <u>won't</u> have any more than two, a boy and a girl; of that I am resolved. But I <u>should</u> have liked to have some little red-haired <u>D</u> boys! – and a little girl like me.

Of one thing I am resolved: I will never fall in love with any other man until I am absolutely certain that he cares for me <u>first</u>! It only brings heart-breakings. A woman is supposed to give her love where it is asked for, and not to love any one on her <u>own</u> account, however secretly. If she does, she must take the consequences of suffering. Men think women are just <u>cows</u>, who can love whoever feeds them well and takes care of their wants! It may be superstitious, but I can't help thinking that if I gave up loving <u>D</u>, he would go down, or some harm might happen to him, even though he does not know I love him.

I sat on the "Lovers' Rock", and read and sewed by turns, and watched the proceedings of Mayor and "Long Anna" (Miss Bennett) and "Friedie" and "Patella" (whose real name is Miss Crystal) all the morning, whilst mother sat on the edge of the rock and read – "Swinsty" was painting just close to mother, and he gave an amused look at me perched upon the rock!

There is an awful story about "Long Anna", as they call that great lanky Miss Bennett, who is always trailing around with Mr Mayor. They say that on Wednesday she went to bathe, with absolutely nothing on, right in front of all the fishermen on the quay!!! (She was bathing from the lifeboat slipway) – and that the big, burly, good-natured looking policeman chased her back to her lodgings, and lectured her severely, as she deserved, – the beast! I wonder how she <u>dare</u>! – when even the <u>coarsest</u> of the Staithes girls will not go down to <u>wade</u>, even on the rocks until dusk! All the little boys feel fully justified now in shouting, "Theer gaws Long Anna!" after her, accompanied by most insulting remarks, and I'm sure I for one, don't blame them! Then they see her going over the far rocks to bathe, even with towels, etc under her arm, they wait until she has got a little way ahead, and then go creeping after her, bobbing down behind rocks and boulders whenever she turns round! I saw them today, doing that.

Whilst I was sitting on the rock, two lovely pantomimes were going on beneath my eyes. First, there was Mayor and Long Anna; L.A. had a picture up on the quay, at which she was looking, and Mayor came up to her, and began to show her how to paint it. Then he got "Patella" to stand a little way off, and he painted her in; she had a most simpering love-lorn expression on her ugly face and looked most grotesque. After they had done with her as a model, she went down on to the beach and stood with a wistful lovelorn expression on her face, looking out to sea, where she was soon joined by "Friedie", and they went together to sit on a projecting rock. They were so engrossed in their conversation, that they did not notice that the tide was rising, until the water was all round them, and one of the two "felleys fra Lunnon", who were watching the scene before them with great amusement, threw a pebble at them. As soon as they became aware of their position, and that everyone was laughing at them, they hopped off the rock, and climbed on to a boat instead, where they were soon joined by Mayor and Long Anna. Mayor put his hand familiarly over "Patella's" two hands, which were lying on her lap, and she then began to stroke and pat his hand. I threw a pebble at mother to make her look up, as she was missing all this, and "Swinsty" looked so mischievous and amused! He <u>is</u> a delightful being! What a pity it is

I sat on The "Lovers' Rock",
and read and sewed by turns,
and watched the proceedings
of ██████ and "Long Anna" and ⁽ᵐⁱˢˢ ᴮ⁾
██████ and "Patella" (whose
real name is Miss ██████)
all the morning, whilst
Mother sat at the side of the
rock, and read. "S██████"
was painting just close to
Mother, and he gave an
amused look at me perched
upon the rock!
There is an awful story
about "Long Anna", as
they call that great
lanky Miss B██████ who
is always trailing around
with Mr. Major. They
say that on Wednesday
she went to bathe, with
absolutely nothing on, right

"LONG
ANNA"
(MISS B█████
(MANCHESTER

he's married! He doesn't seem to care much about his wife, though, nor she about him; I never by any chance see them together. <u>She</u> goes out with the little boys, and sometimes the nursery-governess, and <u>he</u> goes out, chiefly by himself, but often with the governess, and once with one of the little boys – the younger one.

In the afternoon, we sat on the quay, but it grew rather cold and windy, so I put my golf-cape-hood over my head, instead of my hat, and looked like a monk with a cowl. It caused much amusement and interest to "Swinsty", Mayor, the Johnsons and "Mount Moriah", who came to paint quite near us, – a most awful, brilliant daub.

In the evening, we went for a walk to the top of the hill, hoping to meet dear little Riggie, and there, sure enough, I saw him riding towards us on his bicycle! He looked so happy, when he caught sight of me, for I appeared above the crest of the hill before mother, who walks so much slower. He jumped off immediately, and came toward holding out his hand. The Johnsons were just coming up the hill, and they saw it all; Annie Johnson looked so amused, but not disagreeably, so I forgave her, as it was only natural under the circumstances, and what I should have done myself! There was a kind of "Ha!, that's it, is it?" expression on her face, and she looked awfully interested!

R said, when mother said it was time to turn back, "If you'll allow me, I'll walk back with you", so we had his dear little company both ways! He seemed as if he could hardly bring himself to say "goodnight", but the evil moment had to come at last, and he very wisely, did not attempt to see us down the hill, as that would have caused such a frightful amount of gossip in the village. Though I was <u>very</u> sorry to have to part from him so soon, yet I am glad that he did not come down to our door with us. I hope there won't be a talk about us as it is! Staithes can never let other peoples' affairs alone!

Another wet gloomy day. Stayed in all the morning – all the artists went off to play golf or cricket somewhere, and mother and I met them returning about 8.30 in a "conveyance" along the Hinderwell Road. Poor old "Swinsty" has apparently sprained his ankle, or hurt his foot in some way, – no Riggie tonight. Too wet, I suppose. I was much disappointed.

The following article dated Saturday 17th August 1901 was glued into the diary on this page. Presumably the accused was known to Enid.

THE NORTH STAR.

THE ARREST OF MR J. T. HALL.

ARRIVAL IN DARLINGTON.

John Thompson Hall, accountant and stock and sharebroker, who has been extradited from America on five separate charges of having misappropriated sums of money entrusted to him for investment, arrived in Darlington yesterday afternoon, and is now lodged at the police station. Mr Hall's arrival had been anticipated with a good deal of interest, and there was a large crowd on the station platform when he arrived. The case has excited much interest and comment since Hall left Darlington on the morning of the 8th of March last. His movements after that time were something of a mystery, but they are now well known. Hall took a passage in a Cunard liner in the name of "John Francis Harris," stating that he went there as a "transient visitor." After his departure it was discovered that certain sums of money entrusted to him for investment had been

48

misappropriated, and warrants were obtained for his arrest. The amount of the sums misappropriated has been variously stated, but it may be taken that it is not anything like the sum alleged. One of the charges against him is in connection with a Tyne Commissioners' bond of the value of £2,000, which Hall received with instructions to dispose of for a client, but instead of doing so it is alleged he transferred it to his own name, and then mortgaged it for £1,000. He is also charged, at the instance of Dr. Eastwood, of Dinsdale Park, with misappropriating £500 entrusted to him. Hall is also charged with misappropriating £700 the proceeds of the sale of shares in the London and Westminster Bank belonging to the estate of the late Mr Elder, of Eastbourne, Darlington. There is also a further charge of misusing £250, belonging to Mr Aitken, florist, Kirkleatham.

The Public Prosecutor having been called upon to act in the matter, the warrants were sent to New York to the British Consul-General, it having been ascertained, by the receipt of a letter in Darlington, from a man named Mirfin, who was proceeding to an engineering appointment in Mexico, and went out in the same boat, that Hall had landed in the States. He took up his residence with his brother-in-law, at East Orange, New Jersey, and was there arrested by one of Pinkerton's Detective Agency. An application was made for extradition, and Hall was brought to New York for the purpose. Some delay occurred because it was thought that the case was not strong enough against him, and further affidavits and charges were sent out, bringing the number of the latter up to five.

Extradition was eventually granted, and Hall left New York on August 7th in the Germanic, in the custody of Inspector Nairn, of the Metropolitan Detective Police Department, and reached Liverpool on Thursday night. The uncertainty of the time of his arrival in Darlington caused no little excitement among a section of the people. A large crowd waited till midnight on Thursday at Bank Top Station in the hope of seeing Hall on his arrival. They were, however, disappointed. A big crowd assembled again yesterday morning, it being thought that he might arrive by the train reaching Darlington from Liverpool shortly after eleven o'clock, but Hall did not come. The platform was crowded again on the arrival of the 1.49 train, but this, too, had been too early for Hall, and he did not reach Darlington until three o'clock. By this time a great crowd had assembled, and the news soon spread that Hall had arrived. The people travelling by the train had been unaware of the fact, and on its becoming known there was a rush to where Hall stood on the platform with Inspector Nairn, looking after his luggage. Hall appeared to feel his position very keenly. Though he looked pale, there was not much change in his appearance since he left Darlington. It was stated by the American papers that Hall had shaved himself in order to avoid arrest, but there was no trace of this having been the case, and Inspector Nairn, in answer to a reporter yesterday, said Hall looked now as when received into custody.

AT THE POLICE STATION.

As soon as the luggage had been secured, Inspector Nairn called a cab, and drove with his prisoner to Darlington Police Station. The crowd raised a groan as the cab left the station yard. On reaching the police station Inspector Nairn read the warrants over to Hall, who made no reply to the charges. At twenty minutes to four he was brought before Mr James Cox, J.P., in order to be formally remanded. Mr Edward Wooler appeared on behalf of the Public Prosecutor, and Mr Barnley (Middlesbrough) for the prisoner. There were ten reporters present, but none of the public, who were waiting in large numbers at the County Court under the impression that Hall would have been brought up there.

Mr Wooler said he appeared on behalf of the Public Prosecutor, and he had five charges to prefer against the prisoner. The witnesses were very numerous—he had over 30—and he, therefore, suggested that he should simply give formal evidence of arrest, as Hall had only just arrived, and the case could then be adjourned till Tuesday, when he would proceed with two short cases. The court might not be able to sit on Wednesday owing to the room being occupied, but they could sit on Thursday, and proceed day by day till the conclusion.

The Clerk (Mr Newby Watson) said they could arrange to sit on Wednesday.

Mr Cox said they could arrange on Tuesday as to the future sittings of the court.

Mr Wooler replied that he had witnesses to come from Liverpool, Dublin, London, Harrogate, and Newcastle.

There was a large number of them, and he should not like to have them in Darlington until it was necessary. If the court sat on Wednesday it might be very awkward.

The Clerk said he could let Mr Wooler know later whether they could take the case on Wednesday or not.

Mr Wooler said he had to bring witnesses from Dublin, and it was necessary to give them early intimation.

Mr Barnley said he was ready to agree to a remand till Tuesday, and they could arrange a suitable time for proceeding with the case afterwards.

Mr Wooler: Then I will put Inspector Nairn into the box to prove Hall's arrest.

Inspector Nairn was then sworn, and said he had just arrived from New York with the prisoner. He read the warrants in the police station that afternoon, and the prisoner made no reply.

Mr Barnley: I make no objection to the remand till Tuesday. I should like to say, however, that the Press seem to have been very liberal with Hall. The amounts involved has been somewhat multiplied, and it would be just as well if nothing more was said in the papers than has transpired in this court.

Mr Cox: I quite agree with you.

Hall was then remanded in custody till Tuesday next.

Inspector Nairn will, we understand, journey to London to-day, and return to Darlington on Monday night, to be present at the Court on Tuesday.

Mrs Hall visited her husband at the police station about eight o'clock last evening.

August 18th (Sunday) 1901

(This is a mixture of the 18th and the 25th by mistake)

A gloriously fine hot day, after all the rain and gloom. We sat out and read and enjoyed the sunshine (though it was very hot) all the morning, but in the afternoon, as I felt overpowered with sleepiness, I lay on the sofa, and dozed. In the evening, I walked over to Hinderwell Church, arriving about a quarter of an hour late, and finding the place quite full of visitors, with an admixture of natives. I hoped that Riggie would be there, but he was not. However, as I was walking back afterwards, I saw a trim little figure walking along before me, and when I got about a yard behind it, the face turned round with such a happy beam of welcome! I never saw him look so handsome as tonight, I think, dear little boy! – and however did he know that it was I? – for there were heaps of other people, chiefly women, returning along the same road from church. Mother had said that she would meet me at a certain stile, so he and I walked on together till we came up to her. I, in fear and trembling that he should say anything sentimental any minute, and worried about what the people we met might think! – he just looking perfectly happy, but rather shy and quiet, – and so bonny! I kept wondering aloud where mother was, for I felt decidedly uneasy, but he, dear little boy, seemed in no particular hurry to find her, and said that he expected she would be well on her way, though she walked slowly.

When we met her, we stood and talked for a few minutes, and then I proposed that, as we had never been down that path leading round by Dale Houses from the Hinderwell Road, we should leave the beaten track, with its accompaniment of eyes and tongues, and go down that way for a change, to which Riggie fully agreed.

We had rather a scramble to get down, as it was steeper than we had thought, and even Riggie had not thought it was so steep, though he had been down it once before. He was good about helping mother down! She said afterwards that it felt such a strong arm, and a strong heart! Dear little boy! When we reached the bottom of the hill, it suddenly began to rain! The sky had been of a soft, deep dark blue-grey, with copper-colour where the sun had set, but we only thought that it was darkening in for the night, and had not troubled our heads further about it, except to admire the beauty of the quiet evening scene – However, there was a dilemma! We were far from any houses, about half–way between Hinderwell, Staithes and Dale Houses, so that it was equally far to all of those places. Two of us had no umbrellas or mackintoshes, and mother had only a flimsy parasol to cover her nice silk dress and new toque. We made a rush for the hedge, and stood under that for some minutes, hoping that the rain would soon be over. But no such luck! Instead it began to lighten, and the rain came dropping through the hedge on to my thin openwork silk blouse, and it got wetter and wetter. Riggie felt my arm gently, and said "are you getting very wet Miss Robinson?" "Rather, – thank you!" I replied, but there was nothing to be done. I wanted mother to sit down, but instead, she set off giggling in a most idiotic way: I was angry with her, because I thought Riggie would think she was laughing at him, and she would not say what was the matter! Then we all began to giggle till we nearly burst, and nobody had the faintest notion of what it was all about. It appeared afterwards, that mother was under the impression that there was something disagreeable where she was just about to sit, but she persisted in saying that there was an ants' nest there!! There wasn't anything, though, so at last I got mother persuaded to sit down, and then Riggie, who must have guessed at the cause of mother's ill-timed mirth by this time, and who was almost speechless with suppressed laughter himself, said he would go and see if there was any better shelter to be found further along the hedge. He came back in a minute or two from an unsuccessful search, and then mother said I had better put my skirt over my shoulders, if Mr Rigg would excuse it. I demurred at first, as I thought it would look so dreadfully improper, but as I was half-drenched, I at last gave in, and it certainly was warmer and drier. I am only so sorry, because he had nothing of the kind that he could put on. "Are you alright now, Miss Robinson?" he asked "Yes thank you" I replied, "I hope you aren't feeling wet very much?" – "no, I don't mind it if you don't!" he said – "Oh" said I, "I don't mind it at all now, – and I believe you are enjoying it!" – at which he laughed in an embarrassed, conscious way, dear little boy, but did not attempt to deny it! What he did say was, "Oh, I think it's rather exciting, you know! It isn't often one gets adventures like this in a quiet country place like Hinderwell!" – "No" I said, "and we seem fated always to be caught in a storm together, don't we? – at which he laughed innocently "it's quite like a story-book", "Indeed, I continued, it isn't often one gets such adventures <u>out</u> of a novel, is it?" – at which he chuckled quietly to himself for a long time, and at last set <u>me</u> off giggling again! Then the rain began to clear a little, so we emerged like the little Marmots, in the tale that mother used to tell me when I was a baby, and went on our way rejoicing. But we hadn't got further than about a hundred yards, when the rain came on again worse than before, and we were driven to seek shelter under a large Ash tree, and then I went ankle-deep into a ditch! However, I was none the worse, (though my shoes were!) and I felt rather cold and soaked. Then the rain cleared a little, and we stumbled on blindly in the dark, along a cart-road full of ruts, in one of which I slipped, and should have fallen headlong, had Riggie not caught me in his kind strong arm, and pulled me gently out of the way. We passed only one solitary human-being (a miner – I presume) who stopped to look down upon us from the railway embankment where he was walking. I hope he won't tell tales! – but <u>fortunately</u> my skirt was not over my shoulders then, or I don't know what awful gossip might have got about! At last, after more stumbling, we emerged at the coal-wharf near Dale House, and then we knew our way over, so we had a nice slow sweet walk in the cool of the night up Dale House Hill, and back to Staithes, none of us talking very much and R left us at the top of the hill, as usual. Mrs Brown had thought we were in all the time, so had not worried about us, but she was very much startled and astonished when we appeared like drowned rats from the outer world.

August 19th (Monday) 1901

A Lovely day. I hoped that <u>D</u> might come after all, but no! – no sign of him. I think it is pretty clear now that he doesn't care two pins about me, or he could easily have run over, if only for a day. It has cost me untold pain to come to this decision, but <u>having</u> come to it, I don't see the fun of wasting all my heart-love any longer on a person who only throws it back in my face, and probably gives a cynical laugh into the bargain, for love is proverbially blind, and I see and remember things <u>now</u> that I passed over and thought nothing of a fortnight or more ago, – various little neglects and selfishness, and backbiting which I saw and noted, but which I forgave him because I loved him, and because I might have done the same myself. I don't blame poor D for not being able to love me, for it was initially <u>my</u> fault for ever falling in love with <u>him</u>, only I am sorry he hasn't come up to my ideal of what a man, and a <u>gentleman</u> should be! But it was quite my own fault for setting my ideal too high for him to attain to, and I have evidently attached far too great importance to things said merely in a friendly or mildly flirtatious spirit. Poor D, if he would only have loved me a little bit, I would have stuck to him through thick and thin, but as it is, well – that would be merely wasted energy, and perhaps, after all, God knows best, and is guiding me against my will, so I have resolved to think no more about poor D in a sentimental spirit, though, if <u>he</u> makes any advances after this, I shall still be glad to have him as a friend, though not one that I can fully and absolutely <u>trust</u>.

I am beginning to see the hand of providence in all of this, for he would probably have made rather a carping selfish husband, and, at any rate, he would always be liable to be ill, poor fellow, and, though that is chiefly what I loved him for at first, – still, on more mature reflection, – I should not like to spend all of the best part of my life in nursing a fractious invalid! So now I feel in an absolutely unruffled state of mind, except for a vague uneasiness with regard to <u>R</u>, for things are coming on at an alarming rate in that quarter, and I could not bear to hurt his sweet little feelings!

I wrote to father all the morning on the rocks, and read and sewed by turns on the quay in the afternoon. Just as I was going out of our door in the early afternoon, I saw a large crowd coming along the street, with children running and shouting, and somebody shouting in a hoarse, queer voice – I asked little Edie Featherstone what was the matter and she said "It's a man gone <u>mad</u>!" – "gone mad" I ejaculated. "yes, 'e goes mad every full moon and gets hawful drunk!" she replied. I then espied the poor man in question, Neddy Verrill, – a man with sandy hair, a curious round, rather protruding brow, and a dogged, stubborn face, which was now distorted and discoloured by his mad fury and the drink combined, – jumping up in the air with a horrible fiendish laugh, and then grimacing at everybody near him, and running and butting at anyone who came in his way, and also at those who didn't! He disappeared finally up the station road, with a crowd of children laughing at him, and I thought he had gone for good, so mother and I ventured out. We went on to the quay, and were just standing talking to another fisherman named Verrill, who was extremely eager that we should come to the dedication service, or something, in the newly painted Methodist chapel, and was trying to get mother to promise to go and hear Mr Chunn, from Loftus, who was to be the special preacher for the occasion, when suddenly there was a rush, and poor Neddy Verrill came jumping and capering round the corner!

I grabbed mother's arm, and bundled her into Mrs Ward's, neck and crop, and nearly fell on the top of her, so great was my hurry and fright. Then we watched poor Ned out of the window. His brother was amongst the knot of sailors standing by the rails, and he came up to the shouting, grimacing, Ned, and attempted to seize him. Then there was a fearful struggle, in which Ned cursed and fought, and kicked and bit, or attempted to do so, savagely, until he was at last pinned against the wall of a house, and carried away, still struggling by his brother, and several other men. We heard afterwards that he had been put to bed and locked up.

Miss Johnson came up to me, and said she had heard that I did caricatures, and <u>might</u> she see some? – she wanted to see those of all the Staithes artists! I told her that I had left them all at home for safety's sake! – at which she was much disappointed. I asked her who told her? – But she only giggled and blushed!

She then said that Mr Friedie Snr wished to be introduced to me very much, so it must have been <u>he</u> who told her, and <u>R</u>. must have told <u>him</u>! I don't see how he can have got to know otherwise! My fame appears to have spread abroad in the land!

had heard that I did caricatures, and might she see some? — She wanted to see those of all the █████ artists! I told her I had left them all at home for safety's sake! — at which she was much disappointed. I asked her who told her? — but she only giggled and blushed! She then said that Mr. ███ ███ wished to be introduced to me very much, so it must have been he who told her, and R. must have told him! I don't see how he can have got to know otherwise! My fame appears to have spread abroad in the land!

A lovely day, but awfully hot. Father says I may go to Mortola! Jubilate!

I feel now though as though I didn't care for anything or anybody, and I don't feel at all excited about going out to Mortola. I practised on the Institute piano nearly all the morning except for about half an hour, when we sat outside Mrs Thompson's. "Long Anna's" cousin, Miss Bennett, the girl in the flappy white hat, whom Mr Mayor was teaching to paint, – came in to listen to my singing downstairs, and said to mother, "How nicely your daughter sings! I wondered who it was, when I was coming along the street".

"Patella" and "Long Anna" went down to bathe during the morning, and "Patella" sat down suddenly in the dirty green beck! She had nothing on but a white skirt with a mackintosh over, and bare feet!

As I was coming along the High Street in the morning, I saw a poor bullock, half wild with fright, being driven to the butcher's. That would be about 11.30. At 1.30 when mother and I were coming in to lunch, we could not get past for a large crowd and when we got near enough, we saw the poor bullock being dragged by ropes into the slaughter house. The poor thing seemed quite paralysed with fright, and absolutely refused to move. It was a most sickening sight. They whacked it, and shouted at it, and drew the ropes about its neck and horns so tight that its eyes nearly started out of their sockets. At last, a lot of men managed to get a plank shoved under it, and lifted it in bodily. Then there was a scuffle, and it rushed out, and into the shop, where it was finally despatched by three blows from the butcher's hatchet. Mr Bagshawe and a middle aged friend were coming along, and they stayed to watch it, but I heard the friend saying afterwards, "I'm sorry I even saw that much, it's enough to make one feel quite sick", – which was what mother and I felt. We could hardly eat any food after what we had seen.

I sat and read on the "Lover's Rock" in the afternoon, and we walked up the Hinderwell Road with Riggie in the evening.

"Patella"
(Miss C███████
MANCHESTER

A broiling hot day. Sat on far rocks all the morning and read and geologised. Sat near the "ammonite" rock! A faint feeling of sadness of things gone by came over me as I looked at it, but I put these sad memories away from me as I looked at it, and tried to think only of the present. We sat by Mrs Thompson's in the afternoon. There are various new arrivals, including a party of very ugly old maids with a pug dog, but nobody of any interest.

Mayor was painting poor little Anthony Marshall stark naked all the morning, under the blazing sun (M. took great care to have an artist's umbrella!) – for which he gave him only 4d! M painted his sisters waft*.

Walked with R in the evening on Hinderwell Road.

---

*We take this to mean Fred Mayor was painting Anthony Marshall's sisters wafting their brother with a fan.

August 22nd (Thursday) 1901

A broiling day, like yesterday. Read by Mrs Thompson's etc. Ordinary routine – I have lost count of the days entirely, and am writing this up several days after the dates given here. No R in evening – (we found out afterwards that he and a friend had been for a ride to Mulgrave Woods).

A Lovely, hot day. We spent a quiet morning outside Mrs Thompson's cottage, and then Miss Laura Johnson called to us out of her studio window, and asked if we would come up and see some of her work, to which we gladly assented. She paints in the strong "blob-and-dash, I-know-what-I'm-doing" style. I don't care for her pictures much, but liked a sketch of a boy with some small green floats (bladders) very much, and almost thought of buying it, as it was only £4-4-0. But I am glad now that I didn't; I will keep my £4-4-0 for something better, – one of R's for example!

There were Miss Laura Johnson, Miss Lizzie Johnson, Miss Knight, and Miss Gasgoigne and ourselves all there in that small room, in which there was barely room to turn round, so mother had to sit out of the window, on the window-ledge, as she was tired, and there was nowhere else to sit! "Long Anna" and "Patella" were lying full length in two boats on the beach, each with an attendant artist!

Miss Johnson asked us to go to a cricket–match (Artists v. Whitby Visitors – Mr Mayor's team v. Mr Charlie Lyons') at 2.30, and we consented to go, never imagining that this was Friday, – the day we had <u>faithfully</u> promised dear little R. to go and visit him and his dear old mother! What was any cricket-match compared with that! – Well, we went and actually <u>enjoyed</u> the cricket-match, which resulted in a draw.

Our side (the artists) comprised Mr Mayor, Friedie, Knight, Bagshawe, Brown, Richardson, Swinstead, Friedie's brother, a new artist whose name I don't know, a person called "Jones" (who was "chucked in" at the last moment to fill up the vacancy) and another whose name I can't remember.

"Friedie" and "Swinsty" played splendidly, "Friedie" looking just like a little tousled terrier when he ran, – he tore along neck and crop, like a terrier after a rabbit, with his funny billycock (haymaker's) hat off, his arms and legs flashing and flying about in all directions, and his thick brown hair blowing about in the wind.

we went, and actually _enjoyed_ the cricket . match, which resulted in a draw. Our side (the Artists) comprised ▉▉▉▉▉▉, ▉▉▉▉▉, Knight, Bagshawe, Brown, Richardson, S▉▉▉▉▉▉▉▉, I▉▉▉▉▉'s brother, a new artist whose name I don't know, a person called Jones, (who was "chucked in" at the last moment to fill up the vacancy) and another whose name I can't remember.

"▉▉▉▉" and "S▉▉▉▉" played splendidly, "▉▉▉▉" looking just like a little towsled terrier when he ran, — he tore along neck + crop, like a terrier after a rabbit, with his funny billycock (Raymakers') hat off, his arms + legs

running for cricket ball

S____ returning from fielding a ball. (His ankle seemed to give him a good deal of trouble)

M____ nudding-

Knight batting.

Richard-...-son awaiting events.

Bagshawe marching across The field.

Brown preparing to bowl!

"I ____" brother (Hair standing on end)

Jones

The Grand Stand!

When half-time was called, we all trooped into the next field and had an excellent tea (provided by the Miss Johnsons). A loutish Whitby visitor had handed me my tea, "Swinsty" the sugar (and when I said I didn't take it, he said in surprise, "what, <u>never</u>?") – and Miss Johnson, Miss Gasgoigne and Friedie, cakes. Friedie simply beamed upon us when he came round with the cakes and to ask mother if she would have any more tea.

After all this was over, we went back to our ordinary tea, and just when we were in the middle of it, an <u>awful</u> thought came to me! This was <u>Friday</u>, for I remembered seeing Mrs Brown put up the piece of wood with "BANK" in brass letters on the bank room door, before Mr Richardson the banker came! Oh, what a thing we'd done! I turned quite sick at the thought of my poor little boy's disappointment! How <u>could</u> I explain it and make amends! I very nearly cried for vexation, but I yelled out frantically to Mrs Brown, to make quite sure, "Mrs Brown! Mrs Brown! Is it Thursday or Friday?" Her answer came slowly and deliberately, "Why, it's <u>Friday</u>!" I could have eaten my head! I just said to mother, "Get your tea done as quickly as ever you can, and <u>COME</u>! I'm going to get ready!" (It was then 7.35 and we had promised to go by the 3.20 train). When we were ready, I snatched up my music, and tore on ahead to the station to see if there was a train in a few minutes "Not till 8.11 Miss!" said the porter, so, hardly waiting to thank him, I rushed down the station hill, and met mother just coming up the hill from the village. I told her the state of things, and she said that as she walked so slowly, I had better hurry on to Hinderwell and explain, before Mrs Rigg began to go to bed. I simply <u>flew</u> there, – I couldn't have been more than a quarter of an hour, I'm sure! Panting and breathless, I rushed through the village, not daring to ask which was the house, as it looked so suspicious, my going there alone at that hour of the evening! At last, however, I summoned up courage to ask a cart man "which was Mrs Rigg's?" He said 'he didn't know, but he'd ask t'postman', who was sitting on his cart. The postman told me to go to the police-station, and I should find it round the corner. I did this and enquired at the first house round the corner. "No, Mrs Rigg lived a t'other end", so I asked at the last house but one, which had a light in the window, whilst the other was all shut up and dark. "No Miss, Mrs Rigg lives next door". So, in fear and trembling, for it looked as if everybody had gone to bed, I knocked gently. Not a sound. I felt quite shaky now! <u>However</u> was I to explain? I tried to think of something to say, but all my ideas seem to have left me, and my heart was thumping wildly. Summoned up all my courage, and knocked again, this time with my umbrella-handle. I heard a voice, apparently asking "wasn't that a knock?" – and then footsteps, and the door was opened, and there stood the dear little boy with his eyes shining with tears in the faint light – "Oh, what will you think of us? I am sorry!" I gasped – "come in Miss Robinson, won't you?" he said in rather a husky voice. I then tried to explain in rather a broken disjointed way, and between my breathless gasps (for I had not recovered from my race there, and my heart was going 20 to the dozen!) how it had all happened, and meanwhile, the little boy was lighting a large lamp which stood on the table, and the dear old mother came in, and he introduced her. She had told Ernest that he had "made a mull of it, somehow", and she thought he had not made it clear. She thought perhaps father had turned up, or something, and that that had prevented us from coming. Poor dear old lady, she had got a lot of nice little cakes ready for us, and the room smelt deliciously of flowers – Carnations, – and such beauties, too.

Then the sister-in-law, Mrs Alfred Rigg came in, and was introduced, and then R. asked where I had left mother, and said he would go and meet her. I told him not to trouble, – that she would be all right, – but Mrs Rigg said, "Oh, have you left your mother behind? Why, I shouldn't like to be left like that if I'd a daughter, I know! Where did you leave her?" – "Oh, about at the end of the Lane End Houses" I replied – "WHAT!, they all three gasped, nearly as far off as Staithes! Why, she won't know her way here, will she?" – "Oh, she can ask it!" I replied impertinently, "and she'll have to pass by the churchyard!" gasped the dear old lady, "I should be frightened, if I were she!" Then she went on to tell me how terrified she had been when Ernest had been acting as a nigger at the fisher-concert last year, and had had to stay behind to wash the black grease off his face, and she had had to walk nearly the whole way alone – and past the churchyard, too!

Meanwhile, Ernest had gone to meet mother, and he soon returned with her and Mr Jansen, his musical friend, whom he had invited in before, and whom I had met and spoken to in the street, and explained how awfully sorry I was about it all. Mr Jansen had been there all the afternoon, and had only just left when I met him. Poor little Ernest had gone to meet three trains, his mother said! Poor little boy! However, we all cheered up, and had a very jolly, pleasant evening, with plenty of songs, music etc. and the time passed so quickly that we found we had missed the last train, and so we drove back in a "conveyance" and the little boy came to see us down.

August 24th (Saturday) 1901

The black ink has given out, so I am obliged to use red instead.

Another lovely day. We spent a quiet morning in reading, writing, etc. In the afternoon, having promised to go over again to Hinderwell to fetch my music (ostensibly!). We started punctually at 2.30 to climb the hill up to the station, our train leaving at 3.15! Mother insisted on getting there in time, so we started three quarters of an hour before train time, and I took "Eliza" to read in the station, and for <u>him</u> to read afterwards. I couldn't get the carriage door to open, when we reached Hinderwell station, and he hurried up, looking so bonny and sweet and happy, and beaming all over, and with a grand wrench, turned the obstinate handle, and opened the door. He had just been buying a copy of this weeks "Black and White", with a full-page picture, entitled "Comrades", by him, in it, – a little street Arab and his terrier dog, sitting on a doorstep. We walked from the station to his house, looking at this, and talking over the wonderful feats of the man who has been flying round the Eiffel Tower in a new flying-machine.

When we got to his house, we found that it was being painted red on the outside, – to keep it dry. All the nice climbing trees and plants were pulled off the wall, and were hanging in dismal lumps, waving their dishevelled arms in the breeze. There remained, however, one sweet little half-opened tea-rose, which I carelessly and casually remarked on. He immediately said, "Would you like it?" – "Oh," I said, "It's a pity to cut the only one there is!" – and mother and I went into the house, leaving him to cut the rose. He came in with <u>two</u>, he having discovered a bud, somewhere else I suppose. He gave us the choice, and mother chose the half-blown one, (which I had wanted!) and I the bud. Mother gave as her reason for choosing the fuller blown one, that "a bud was more like a young girl!" – We sat and talked for some time after that, and then he asked me to play or sing, so I first played Allan Macbeth's lovely Intermezzo, "<u>Forget me not</u>", and the song "<u>Lascia ch'io pianga</u>" and "<u>Sleep, my Love, Sleep</u>". After the first, he said "you must play a great deal, then, to yourself, without the music, – from memory, – don't you, Miss Robinson?" – "Oh, yes, I do", I replied, " – I often sit and play to myself in the dark to soothe my nerves when they are jangled and upset!" – at which he seemed amused. He liked "<u>Lascia</u>" very much, and said it suited my voice admirably, but I think he liked "<u>Sleep, my Love, Sleep</u>", the very best, for he went out of the room, shortly afterwards, to look for something, humming the tune softly to himself, and he did not say much, except a deep "<u>Thank you</u>!" when I had finished singing it. It is a lovely song, and very affecting – Everybody loves it – I never met one who didn't, even though the words are decidedly passion-laden, and might not appeal to everybody!

Then "Lily" (Mrs Alf. Rigg) came in, and we grew more prosaic. Mother says she gave a most amusing sort of wink, or knowing look, over my head (which I, of course, did not see!) – as much as to say, "Ha! So you've got her at <u>last</u> Ernest!" He looked decidedly uncomfortable, mother says, and blushed very much, and then frowned at 'Lily' with a sort of "You – shut up!" expression, which however, had very little effect on the irrepressible "Lily", who smiled all the more!

They gave us tea out of Ernest's exquisite china tea-set, real old Sevres, I should say, and perfectly <u>lovely</u>! The dear old lady said with such pride that all those tea-things were Ernest's, but that he <u>would</u> keep them locked up in the cupboard, out of sight, and he would never have them used! (They were used for <u>us</u> though!) – that cupboard was far too small to hold them, and it wasn't worthwhile having glass doors put to it, because of the expense, but that "ERNEST SHOULD DO AS HE LIKED, <u>WHEN HE WAS MARRIED</u>!", – putting great stress on the last few words! I really believe there is something in the air, but I can't for the life of me see how I am to prevent the final blow! I <u>am</u> so sorry, if my ideas should prove to be right, – but anyway, I can't help it, for whenever I <u>have</u> done anything in the way of squashing him, he has looked so miserable, that his dear face, and beautiful eyes have <u>haunted</u> me, until I have made him look happy again! My <u>poor</u> little boy! I would give <u>anything</u> to save him from unnecessary pain, but I sadly fear that if things continue at this rate, it is absolutely inevitable! When we left, we went in a conveyance (the last train having left ages ago!) and he again came to see us down to our door.

I was so afraid there would be a knot of sailors standing at the corner as usual, but they seemed all to have gone to bed. I said I was afraid they would set gossip afloat, and he said rather sadly, "Well, would you rather I didn't come down with you?" – "Why, what nonsense!" I said – "It isn't you, of course", (it was, though!) "It's the lateness of the hour, and our being out so late, that I'm afraid will cause gossip!" However, there weren't any sailors, so it was all right, and Mrs Brown did not see him come down with us, so that was all right too!

August 25th (Sunday) 1901

It was fine in the morning and afternoon. Rain at night (see August 18th). Mother and I went to the Primitive Methodist Chapel in morning, in accordance with mother's promise to the red-haired Verrill, who afterwards came up, and, nearly shaking our hands off our arms, said, "<u>wull missus, ah'm verra glahd ter see yer boath</u> 'ere!" – punctuating each word with a violent shake of the hand! – We heard a very nice "dedication sermon" from a Mr Chunn, of Loftus, – a <u>vast</u> improvement on that idiotic, stuck–up Mr Warburton! – who afterwards came up to us, as we were waiting for the crowd to get out, and said, "How do you do? Are you staying here?" We both felt rather startled, and looking a one another said, "Er – quite well thank you, – Yes!", – "Where?" – was the next question, "at Mrs Brown's, the Bank!" I replied, feeling driven into a corner, by this unexpected inquisitiveness, "Oh, yes!" – then after a pause – "You're <u>Mrs Phillips</u>, aren't you?" – turning to mother! – "Oh, <u>no</u>!" said mother, with consternation in her tones! – "Oh, I <u>beg</u> your pardon!, I thought you were!" said the poor man, looking much confused. He then went out at the door, and we waited for a minute or two, to let him get out of the way, and then followed suit, but there he was, waiting for us outside!! This was more than we had bargained for! We were obliged, therefore, to walk as far as Mrs Brown's with him, though it was much against the grain, and I was afraid that "Swinsty" might be looking out of his window, and might take us for Methodists! We took the earliest opportunity of informing poor Mr Chunn that we were church people. Mother said, "That first hymn you had this morning was rather like one of our <u>church</u> hymns!" "Oh" said Mr Chunn, taken aback, "Er, you go to church then!" "Yes", we replied, and mother carefully explained how we came to go to chapel that morning. Soon after, Mr Chunn politely took leave of us, for which we were very glad, though he was a pleasant, unassuming sort of man, and quite well-informed and educated for a dissenting minister!

We made careful enquiries about "Mrs Phillips", and found that she was the person with whom Mr Chunn was to get his dinner, and that she lived down the Coastguard's Yard. Needless to say, mother was utterly disgusted at being taken for a person in that walk of life, however worthy! "Houf! Umph! the idea of taking <u>me</u> for <u>that</u> person!" was all she could say!

In the evening, I went to Hinderwell Church, and the events transpired which I have recorded by mistake under the heading of August 18th.

A Cold, dull, cheerless morning, which ripened into a violent northern gale in the afternoon and evening.

The first exhibition of the "Staithes Art Club" <u>was</u> to have been opened in the afternoon, at about half past two, or a quarter to three, but there wasn't any definite opening, on account of the storm. – First of all, we heard that it was to be opened at 1.30 by Mr Bagshawe's fiancée, Miss Turnbull, from Whitby, then that it would be opened at 2.30 by the <u>Duchess of Kent</u>! Mother said that it would be much more likely to be the "Duchess of Bagshawe", and this proved to be the case in the end!

Well, after hearing such conflicting reports, and as nobody seemed to know anything about it, I asked Mr Neashaw, whom I saw disappearing in at the institute door. "Nay, <u>ah</u> deeunt knea!" he said, "but, ere's misther Bagshawe a-comin'; ah'll ax 'im, though ah bet anything 'e won't knea '<u>isself</u>, though it's '<u>im</u> as is a-gettin' of it oop!" So he asked Mr Bagshawe, whom, by the way, I consider an unmannerly young man, <u>and</u> then later, without troubling to raise his cap, said in an off–hand tone, addressed half to me and half to Mr Neashaw, "Oh, about half–past two, or a quarter to three!" – and then turned on his heel and moved off! (He was very rude or rather gauche about some forms at the cricket–match; mother & I were sitting on a form, there were a number of "Whitby Visitor" girls (Misses Lyon, I presume) on the same form, and he came up and said, "let me move this form into the shade for you!" and took hold of it, with that intention, without ever apologising for disturbing mother and me! It was very thoughtless to say the least of it, but then, the average young man of the present enlightened age, is not blessed with an over plus of manners!).

Well, to continue about the exhibition, I told mother what Mr Bagshawe had said, and we sat in our outdoor things during lunchtime, and waited until the Duchess of Kent, or her substitute should arrive. Meanwhile, the storm increased in fury, and as nothing happened before 4 o'clock, and I saw several people going into the Institute, I

August 26th (Monday) 1901.

. A cold, dull, cheerless morning, which ripened into a violent Northern gale in the afternoon and evening. The first Exhibition of the "Staithes Art Club" was to have been opened in the afternoon, at about half-past two, or a quarter to three, but there wasn't any definite opening, on account of the storm. — First of all, we heard that it was to be opened at 1.30 by Mr Bag-shawe's fiancée, Miss Turn-bull, from Whitby; then, that it would be opened at 2.30 by the Duchess of Kent! Another said it would be much more likely told mother I thought the exhibition must be open, and, if she would supply me with the modest sum of 2d, I would go and investigate. I just managed to get outside the door, and then was nearly blown down as could be! The wind was really awful!

(The black ink has come, so I can go on writing as usual)

Looking up the street, I saw a familiar, dapper little figure coming down it, accompanied by a stouter figure in a drab Norfolk suit. Both beamed all over at me, and I did the same at them, though the wind kept us apart for some seconds. When at last we managed to get up to one another, R. began, "How do you do Miss Robinson, it's very windy isn't it?" (This whilst we were shaking hands) – then, turning to the beaming faced, roundabout figure in the drab Norfolk suit, "I don't think you know _____", but there the wind stopped all further attempts at an introduction by blowing all three of us violently apart! R. was blown across the street nearly into the "Loftus Co–operative Stores", the brother (for such I rightly divined him to be) was blown some way down the street into a doorway, and I was hurled against Mrs Brown's Bank – room window! It was a wonder I didn't break it, for I was blown against it with considerable force! However, after one or two fruitless efforts, and a considerable amount of laughter, we managed to come together again, and then R. shyly asked if I would go with them to the exhibition as mother was too afraid of the wind to venture out – I asked mother, and as she could not very well say "no" whilst they were there, she rather hesitatingly agreed, and I went.

We had a good look round the pictures before anyone else arrived, and R. kept very close to me, and murmured comments in a delightful low voice, whilst his brother Alfred stared fixedly at one thing after another with his back turned towards us – (I am inclined, on further reflection, to think that this was by design, and that he had been "primed" to do it by R.!) – Soon, however, that horrid monkey, Mayor, spoilt everything by running up three steps at a time, and gazing at our little party open mouthed, and in a suspicious sort of way – nasty beast! What business has he to spy on us, I should like to know, especially after his own carryings–on!

Presently, however, Mr Brown, Mr Bagshawe, and a whole troupe of men, came up, so I said quietly to R. "See, I'm the only girl here! I think I'd better go!" – where upon he said, "might he see me back to Mrs Brown's?" I felt obliged to say "yes", because he is such a perfect dear, and looks so hurt when I refuse these requests, but, Oh dear! I'm sure I am "in for it" now, unless we can get away before – well, we are so involved, now, that there <u>can</u> be but one end to it all!! ____

Mother asked him and "Alfred" to come in, and have tea with us, later, so I went out again for a tea-cake or two, and not very long after, we all sat down to tea together, – "Alfred" is a most lively specimen, but <u>very</u> common! – he is, however, a very kind-hearted, and well-intentioned little man, but oh, what a difference he presents to his brother! <u>He</u> is certainly the "flower of the family", dear boy! –

After tea, as it began to rain violently, they looked at my drawings, books, etc (Bell's handbooks to the old masters, – "VELASQUEZ" and "Corregio", – took their fancy immensely, – especially "Velasquez", which I lent to R. to read at his leisure).

I am beginning to be really frightened about dear little R., for I could see that he was tremendously affected by my presence, – and, indeed, I always am by <u>his</u>, now! – and oh, where will all this lead to! I am afraid he will be <u>miserable</u> when we leave Staithes! I'm sure <u>I</u> shall be, little as I ever expected such a thing! – I cried myself to sleep at night.

A gloriously fine day, with a tremendously strong wind, and a splendid sea, – the waves dashing quite over the houses in the coast-guards yard, – about 30ft high, – mother and I sat on the slipway, watching them and were presently joined by old Joe Verrill, who, pointing in a mysterious way at two tripper-like men close by said, "noo, then! Can yer tell meh whaur them two cooms fra'? Eh?" – I smilingly replied, "no, I can't!, can you?" – "ahy!" replied old Joe, knowingly, "ah kens mair'n yow, anny'ow! Ah ken weel enow whar theh cooms fra'!" – "How?" I asked. "whoy, by t'coot o' the'r jib!" said old Joe, as if implying, what a baby you are to ask such a question! – "how do you mean?" said I, puzzled – Joe leant a little nearer – "what'll yer gie meh, if ah's raight? – Eh?" – with a nudge – "I don't know!" I said smiling – "well!" he said, "Ah'll bet theh' nounce-'er-terbahccer that they cooms fra' Lunnon! Will yer tak't? – Hey!" he proceeded to call to the two men in question, but I at once shut him up with, "Oh, hush! Don't! you mustn't attract their attention like that, really! I can't have it!" – at which old Joe nearly died of laughter – and when at last he could speak, he exclaimed, "Ah've doon yer! Eh, Ah've doon yer now! – and mind yer 'aves may a ounce-er-terbahccer, an' ah lahikes it thrupp'ny shag, – ay, a nounce-er-thrupp'ny shag! Haw-haw-haw! (slapping his knees) Ah've doon yer fahine! Whoy, ah axed em this marnin', afoor ah see'd yow, whar theh coomed fra' an' yon feller in t'knee–britches, e ses ter me, 'e ses, "Way coom fra Lunnon, way do!" now ah've doon yer, aven't ah?" I quite owned that he had "doon" me "fine" and later in the day, I caused Mr Featherstone's beaming visage to beam to its widest extent by asking for "threepenny worth of shag – an ounce of threepenny shag tobacco, please!" – "are yer going' ter smoake it yerself, Miss Rob'ns'n?" he enquired, with a benevolent grin, whilst his daughter went off into a fit of laughter! I took it to old Joe at once, and he then said, rather contritely, "Aw, noo, yer knaw, ah didn' mean thaht yer wuz really ter git meh 'nouncerterbahccer!, it wuz oanly mah joake! Eh, wull, it's varry god on yer, an' ah gives yer me best thahnksfur't! – Ay, thahnk yer, Miss Robbis'n!" I think the old fellow was pleased anyway.

Sitting in the bright, hot sunshine, watching the monotonous recurrent "bomb-b-sh-h-h!" of the huge waves, as they thudded against, and broke over the sea-wall and houses, and the scurrying roar of the backwash, had given me a baddish headache, so I lay on the sitting-room sofa at Mrs Brown's all the afternoon and finally fell asleep. When I woke up, in time for tea, I felt much better and inclined for a walk along the Hinderwell Road in the evening, so mother and I set out, and, ere long, were met by R., who turned and walked nearly to Hinderwell with us, and then came back again! As we were returning, mother feeling rather tired, we went up and leant over the gate at the top of the steep field about half-way between Staithes and Hinderwell. The moon was rising, and a soft white mist enveloped the woods nearby, at the bottom of the decline. Various shapeless white masses (sheep) were dotted about the field. The road behind us was perfectly quiet, save for occasional strolling pairs of lovers, – and a deep peace pervaded all things, ourselves included. R. and I did not talk much; we felt instead! I am certain, now, that he is deeply in love with me, – but what a terribly awkward situation! Poor, dear, little R! If only we can get away back to Darlington without his proposing, and so giving me the misery of paining him, by refusing him, – which I shall have to do, for I see no other way out of it! And yet, I have actually, in spite of myself, and my passion for D, and my position and everything, grown to love R. too dearly, for me to dare to think of wounding him in any way! What a state of affairs are we coming to! I feel so fearfully perturbed about it all! – A pair of lovers came along the road, and stopped (unaware of our presence) to kiss close to us, and then R. and I looked at one another, and both laughed in an embarrassed, conscious way, whilst mother tried to relieve the situation by making silly remarks about the sheep and the view!

Another fine, windy day. During the morning and afternoon, mother and I watched the glorious, big waves dashing over the houses again, from "The Goal of all the Saints", and from opposite old Joe's cottage. In the evening, just as we were starting out for our usual walk, we met R. coming down the hill towards Mrs Brown's. It was too windy for him to cycle down, so he had walked, instead, and had brought with him a bundle of "Phil May's Comic Annuals", and the book, also illustrated by Phil May, which Mr Elton mentioned to me, "The Parson and the Painter", and also my confession album, which he took away with him on Monday, as I had asked him to write in it. We asked him to kindly leave them at Mrs Brown's – or at least, he proposed that he should do so, whilst we waited for him, and then we all walked together up the Hinderwell Road. Really, I do wonder what the natives think of all this though! It is, unfortunately, well that we are leaving Staithes on Saturday! I feel quite reckless now, and mean to enjoy things whilst I can, and let him enjoy our society too, and things must take their own course after that! "Apres nous, le deluge!" – and it <u>will</u> be a deluge, too; so much so, that I tremble to think of it, and so put it weakly from me, and only dare to face the immediate present!

We met "Mayor" and "Friedie", who stared decidedly rudely – at least Mayor did: I suppose he thought how soon I had forgotten D! I do reproach myself sometimes for this, but I can't help it; it was his own fault for not coming when I expected him, and now I don't care a lot for him, since my love for R. is of a much truer, deeper kind, founded in unselfish sympathetic sorrow, instead of in selfish joy –

This morning, whilst I was dressing, before breakfast, I heard voices below in the sitting-room, and then mother's voice called up the stairs, "Enid, be quick! Here's Mr Rigg!" I was flabbergasted, of course, and called back, "All right! wait a minute, I'm coming!". I couldn't, for the life of me, imagine what he could have come about, unless _____!

But there was no time to think of any possible explanation of this early visit, so I scuttled down-stairs as quickly as possible, and I entered the room, I called out "Well, good morning Mr Rigg! aren't I late!" (it was then just 10 o'clock!) He looked at me with the sweetest smile, and a sort of adoring look, but I noticed that his eyes were full of tears, though he attempted to reply gaily, "Oh, well, perhaps you aren't always quite so late, Miss Robinson!" – I made some common place reply, in a light tone, but I was feeling very anxious, and wondering what could have happened, to make the dear fellow look like that – However, presently it all came out – Mother began: "Mr Rigg kindly called to see if you and I could go to Lythe Flower Show, and then on to see the Mulgrave Woods, near Whitby, which he says are very beautiful, – but I tell him that I am afraid father would not at all approve of it, and that we must wait until some time that he can come with us, too!" (This was her way of getting out of the difficulty; quite a tactful one, considering).

Poor little R! My heart felt as if it would twist for pity, for he looked so miserable, and yet so sweetly trustful in mother's goodness, and resigned to the inevitable.

His beautiful mournful dog's eyes were all brimming and wet with unshed tears, and conversation, under these circumstances, was very difficult. I longed to comfort him, as one would a child, but could not find anything except trivialities to say! I am only just beginning to realise how very, very much I do love him. His presence has always had an extraordinary effect on me, – far worse than that produced by D's, because D. intended to excite me, in a quiet and insidious way, whereas R. is above all machinations of that sort! Dear, little pure–minded man that he is! Perhaps that is partly why he feels <u>my</u> presence so much, too, – (for I know he does!) – simply because his appetite is not cloyed with illegal passion, and innumerable women.

A very rainy, cold day, but better in the afternoon, and misty in the evening.

R. had asked us to go there this afternoon and evening, before we leave tomorrow, as a sort of farewell visit. It was a very <u>mournful</u> occasion, though we all did our level best to make it otherwise. Poor, <u>dear</u> little R. was very visibly affected, and when he was cutting some bread for us for supper, the tears were shimmering on his eyelashes in the lamp light, and he looked up at me with his <u>beautiful</u>, faithful dog like blue eyes so full of pain, that it was all I could do to keep from crying myself, and knowing all, I had a great lump in my throat, and could hardly speak. I felt perfectly wretched, in fact, seeing him in such a state.

We managed to get through a few songs, however, and he sang "Long ago in Alkala"; and "Under the Circumstances" and "When I was a Boy at School", to try to cheer things up a little. As we were leaving the house, finally, I quietly dropped my little embroidered handkerchief for him to find and keep as a memento if he liked, dear little fellow!

A fine morning, which we mostly spent in, finishing our packing. Mother had asked dear little R. to lunch, and she very tactfully left us to ourselves for a few minutes, for, as she told me afterwards, she saw that the inevitable was coming, and she thought it would be better to get it over, for both of us, so she left him a chance. He did not utilize that particular chance, however, and mother gathered this much, when she returned, by our faces, she said!

I felt horribly nervous and awkward when we were thus left alone together, and a sort of longing seized me to stave off the inevitable at any price, so I chattered and laughed in the wildest fashion, sixteen to the dozen! R. hardly said anything, but just gazed and smiled in blissful contentment!

Then, mother came in and we had lunch, and discussed the merits of plums, raw or stewed! – and he told us of some alterations that his mother was having to make in some cottages belonging to her in Bradford.

Then we went out for some final shopping, and to bid goodbye to all our fisher-friends, – R. and I, that is; mother had not quite finished her packing, so remained at home to finish it. R. bought me some rather green pears, – the best that Staithes could produce – "for the journey", and when mother saw these, afterwards, she caused me much shame and awkwardness by saying (without in the least knowing that they were a present from R.!) "Oh, what horrid green pears! Couldn't 'she' have got any better ones!" I, blushing furiously, was obliged to say, "You don't understand, mother! They're a present!" Poor mother was much mortified, then, to find what she had done, but it was a truly awkward and uncomfortable moment for all of us! Poor, dear little R. looked rather hurt, but, then, knowing it was entirely unintentional on mother's part, he shyly laughed it off, which was very kind of him.

After the shopping, we went to sit at "The Goal of all the Saints", as this is a quiet spot, though well within view – I wondered if "it" would happen here, but he didn't seem inclined to talk much.

Some embarrassingly <u>naked</u> little boys started bathing right in front of our eyes, from the lifeboat slipway. I felt distinctly uncomfortable till R. gave rather a nervous, shy, little laugh, and then, as they were only <u>children</u>, we both laughed openly, and I said I thought people made a great deal too much fuss about these sort of things, and were far too easily shocked, as the Davises were, at all the little naked babies and boys about Staithes. "Oh, I'm glad you feel like that, too, Miss Robinson!" he said "after all, it's natural, and they're <u>made</u> like that, and <u>God</u> made us <u>all</u>!" He takes such pure, natural views of things, dear little man. After that, my temporary embarrassment vanished, and we talked of other things, but soon after, we rose to go, as it was getting near to our train–time. I called his attention to "Wharepuni" and in so doing, touched his arm slightly, and the instant my hand rested on his sleeve (only for a moment) I heard him draw in his breath with a great choking sort of gasp!

When we arrived at the house, I found that mother and the luggage-cart (driven by "Bobby" Atkinson) had gone on before, so after saying "goodbye" to Mrs Brown and the children, I joined R. again and we started to walk up the steep hill to the station. I heard his breath coming in quick, panting gasps, but supposed that it was only the steepness of the hill which was causing this! However, when we had nearly reached the top, he turned to me with a look of happy pride and <u>exaltation</u> all over his dear face, which I shall <u>never forget as long as I live</u>, and said "I should feel it such an honour if I could become <u>engaged</u> to you, Miss Robinson".

My heart leapt into my throat, and I was trembling all over at this, my first proposal! I could not answer him at once, for such a tide of mingled feelings swept over me, and, for a moment, I almost thought I should have <u>fainted</u>, though I never did such a thing in my life! Anyway, I gulped and nearly choked with suppressed emotion! And he was looking so confident and happy, the darling, and beaming down on me with such a <u>protecting</u> look on his dear face!

As I did not answer, he continued, "If I could only <u>correspond</u> with you, Miss Robinson, it would be the happiest time of my life! I have such a <u>very</u> high opinion of you, – in fact <u>the</u> very <u>highest</u> opinion, and I'm sure <u>no</u> man could have a higher opinion of you than <u>I</u> have!"

I could only say, "Oh, Mr R., I don't know <u>what</u> to say to you! I don't <u>indeed</u>! I don't know <u>what</u> my father will say to it all, and I'm awfully afraid he won't approve of it! Oh, I <u>wish</u> it hadn't come about! but, oh, Mr R. I have tried to prevent it and I <u>hope</u> you don't think I've tried to flirt with you!"

"No, indeed!" cried he indignantly, "I've <u>far</u> too high an opinion of you ever to think <u>that</u>, so please don't even <u>suggest</u> such a thing!"

How I reached the station, I don't know, for my movements after that were entirely mechanical. We met mother on the platform, and there was just time to jump into the train, and then to say "goodbye"

At the last moment, a big, grimy paw was thrust into our window, and the shrewd, humorous, kindly face of old Joe Verrill twinkled up at me. "Hey!" said he "Ah's coom ter say 'Goodbye' ti yer!" cried he as the train moved off, waving his peaked sailor's cap. What, I answered, I know not, for I was absolutely dazed, and living in a dream. Besides, I felt fearfully annoyed with poor kindly old Joe, for the moment, for spoiling R's and my goodbye! I smiled at R. tearfully over old Joe's head, whilst I was talking to old Joe, and then R. walked along by the side of the rapidly-quickening train, and we gripped hands, and I had only just time to say to him low enough for his ears alone, "<u>Well, goodbye, and TRY NOT TO WORRY, WHATEVER HAPPENS!</u>" My last sight of his dear face and figure was of him, waving his "yachting" cap in farewell, from the end of the platform. Then I sat back and abandoned myself to my thoughts, and hardly spoke to poor mother the whole way. She merely asked me, "well, has he proposed?" and when I shamefully said "Yes!" she smiled, and said, "I thought so, by your two faces!"

Oh, what <u>will</u> father say! How <u>angry</u> he will be! He'll say it's all that d____ Staithes! – and it's the fault of mother, for going to a small place like that, and letting me "get mixed up with all those d_____d artist-fellows!".

Poor little R! How sweet he looked, and how <u>can</u> I ever bear to hurt his dear feelings, and bring that "whipped-dog" pleading expression into those <u>beautiful</u> blue eyes, and worse still, <u>tears</u>! I must try to collect my thoughts, and consider all the "pros and cons" and weigh all the reasons for and against our marriage.

I put them down here for clearness' sake.

Points in Favour	Objections
1. <u>Perfect</u> character	1. <u>Yorkshire (Bradford) accent</u> (I fear insuperable!)
2. Handsome face.	
3. Sticks to work	2. <u>His</u> relations, – that awful <u>Lily</u>, & his brothers!
4. Very fond of me.	
5. I'm very fond of him.	3. What would <u>my</u> relations think of it all?
6. <u>Perfectly</u> sound & healthy	
7. A <u>true gentleman</u> at heart.	4. It would mean ostracision by all my former friends.
8. Very good to his Mother	
9. No conceit about him.	5. Poverty, – only £300 or £400 a year at <u>most</u>.
10. Plays the piano [& sings very nicely]	6. Position, – nowhere, compared with my <u>present</u> position.
11. Perfectly honest and straight forward	
12. Very sympathetic	7. Doesn't read much.
13. Paints beautifully	8. Mind not sufficiently <u>cultivated</u> (not <u>cultured</u>) to be a true mate for mine
14. Has known sorrow and suffering	
15. Has some very nice possessions, – pictures, china, old furniture etc	9. Dullness of country (I hate the country, except in spring and early summer)
16. Old enough not to be silly, and to be a true protector.	10. Not fond of society and entertainments!
	11. Thirteen years older than me. 21 in 1889... 31 in 1899...33 in 1901

A photograph of Staithes Beck by John Valentine circa 1890.

STAITHES. 4.507. J.V.

89

R

ERNEST. H. RIGG. Esq.

Ernest Higgins Rigg from Enid's
caricature and drawing books of Staithes' characters in 1900.

THE DIARY

A reflection by Darnley Rigg, daughter of Ernest Higgins Rigg.

I was very pleased to be presented with a copy of this diary by James Hart, whom I already knew after a chance meeting during one of his holidays near my home.

Needless to say, I'm very glad that the romance between my father and Enid Robinson fizzled out, otherwise I would not be writing to you today! My father married quite late in life and when I was a child, and he in his fifties, like many artists he relocated to warmer climes near Salcombe in Devon, where I still live.

On first reading the diary, my feelings were that Enid's comments, such as they are, show her tendency to live in a romantic dream world, plus a conventional and rather conditioned outlook, which if she was older, one could consider patronising. The picture she paints of a tedious wimp with permanently welling eyes and spaniel-like devotion does not resemble the father I knew. Her seeming obsession with height seems rather exaggerated, 5'10" not being abnormally small, especially then. On further reflection, their meeting was essentially a holiday romance with all the heightened emotion it involves, and Enid was at an age where she would have been prone to romantic day-dreaming and over dramatising the story for better effect, more because of her upset with 'D'. The text needs to be viewed in context with the customs and etiquette of the day, and as events are so long ago, I'm sure I can forgive and forget.

That said, I think Enid's diary extremely well written and understand she went on to raise a family rather than develop her talents professionally, as did many women in those days, which is a shame.

My memories of him, include a man wrapped up in, and dedicated to his work, of a serious turn of mind, though he could be sociable and animated when the occasion called for it. In fact, so few of his paintings were executed in Staithes, I assume he prefered socialising rather than working whilst he stayed there! A good pianist, I recall that he usually played for me when I went to bed as a child. He was essentially practical and able, on occasion mending his boots with the proper tools and a cobblers' 'last'. Also dismantling and repairing clocks.

Although I'm sure he had an emotional side, I would describe him as quite a stern, strict man. He applied himself diligently to his painting and was interested in his art in a comprehensive way. I have only just cleared his outbuilding studio of many bundles of art journals and periodicals which have remained untouched since he died in 1947.

He was not worldly in the sense of money matters or social life, which did not interest him, his two artist and Bradford gallery-owning brothers; Arthur and Alfred, were much more socially orientated. I never knew them.

The Staithes, Runswick and Hinderwell days and nights were happy and informal times, with musical evenings and concerts in the local halls. I also have earlier information about his student days at the Académie Julian in Paris and varnishing days at the Royal Academy where he exhibited large paintings for twenty years. I have records of these.

All said, I was pleased that the diary confirmed what a caring man he was and it was very moving for me to be put back in touch with him.

Darnley Rigg

Staithes Harbour – Valentine Series *(There is an artist with easel lower left).*

A photograph of Runswick Bay by John Valentine circa 1890. *(Note the artist's white parasols).*

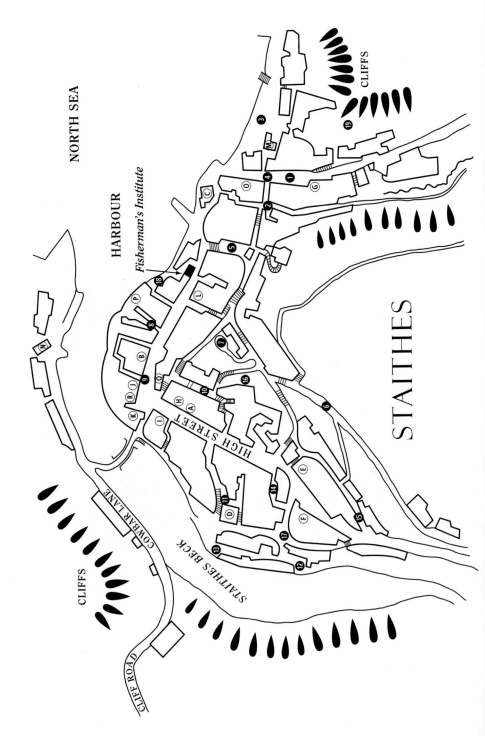

STAITHES

NORTH SEA

HARBOUR

Fisherman's Institute

CLIFFS

CLIFFS

HIGH STREET

STAITHES BECK

COWBAR LANE

CLIFF ROAD

94

PLAN – KEY

(A) The Black Lion
(B) The Royal George
(C) The Cod & Lobster
(D) Wesleyan Chapel
(E) Primitive Chapel (Staithes Museum)
(F) Bethel Chapel
(G) St Peter's Chapel
(H) The Gift Shop
(I) Post Office
(J) Staithes Gallery
(K) The Coble Cafe
(L) Butcher's Shop
(M) Beach Cafe Toilets
(N) Life Boat House
(O) Captain Cook Cottage
(P) The Watch House
(Q) Telephone
(R) Mrs Brown's Bank House

1 Church Street
2 Gunn Gutter
3 Seaton Garth (The Staith)
4 Dog Loup
5 The Barras
6 The Old Stubble
7 Mount Pleasant
8 Boathouse Yard
9 Barbers Yard
10 Broomhill
11 Chapel Yard
12 Beckside
13 Granary Yard
14 Elliots Yard
15 Browns Terrace
16 Darlington Terrace
17 Bob Bells Bank
18 Garth Ends
19 The Lookout

Staithes Beck taken by Victorian photographer Graystone Bird. An artist and inquisitive child can be seen under the trestle bridge. Also, the 700ft long 152 ft high railway bridge spanning the gorge in the distant mist. Photograph supplied by the Keasbury-Gordon Photograph Archive.

STAITHES

Much has been written about Staithes' history and its impressionist art colony which flourished in the later part of the 19th century and first decade of the 20th century, known collectively as the 'Staithes Group'. Many excellent books of reference are available on these subjects and are listed on page 101, though a brief introduction is necessary for the unacquainted.

The village of Staithes, once considered a town, is situated in a valley on the North Yorkshire coast, with steep cliffs on each side. The houses in 1901 were primitive dwellings with red pan-tiled or thatched roofs, but little has changed since. The native inhabitants were a hardy and yet strangely aloof breed, reputedly descended from a race of Norsemen who were wrecked along the rocky coastline in earlier centuries. This insular race of people did not usually welcome strangers, even those from neighbouring villages, so the coming of the railway and its travellers must have heralded an era of accelerating change.

The importance of the railway.

With the opening of the Railway between Saltburn in the North and Whitby to the South in 1883, it became much easier for visitors to reach this remote coastal outpost. Staithes started to attract more and more leisure visitors, who now had a relatively fast and trouble free means of exploring farther afield. Staithes was also 'big news' in this country's many art schools such as Nottingham, Slade and Bushey. Many of the artists who travelled to the area were well trained, often abroad at schools such as the Antwerp Academy in Belgium and Académie Julian in Paris. Nottingham School of Art tutor Thomas Barrett, who owned a holiday cottage in Staithes, spread the word encouraging a steady flow of professional and hopeful amateur artists to visit villages such as Staithes in the North East and Newlyn in the South West of England. Other trippers simply painted as a hobby in much the same way as people take photographs today.

Staithes and Runswick Bay, with their steep cliffs, quality of light, higgledy piggledy houses crammed up and down narrow alleyways, and fishing industry were ideal subjects for these artists seeking to paint and record a fast disappearing rustic way of life, away from the machinery and smoke of the fast industrialising towns. These very artists and other visitors often sought board, lodgings, studios and models, consequently a fledgling economy started to grow; the seedling tourist industry which is so important to the area today. The artists were soon accepted and respected.

Before the mobile phone.

One can only imagine how the Staithes artists must have struggled to make a living from their chosen career. Creating beautiful works of art must have only been half the battle. Much of the demand for their work was cultivated in the wealthy industrial towns such as Leeds, Bradford and Manchester. It was essential for the ambitious artists to forge links with well-heeled industrialists and mill owners from the northern towns, many of whom would be looking to adorn their mansion walls with impressionistic paintings depicting rustic life on the Yorkshire coast.

The card below reads as follows:

> *Can you spot Freedie here? Write here, the boys are here but we leave on Saturday, so write Friday at the latest.*

> Verso: *Hinderwell Jan 6 1904 (Wednesday). Are you at home next Monday? If so I will run over and see you if quite convenient. Yours A.C.*

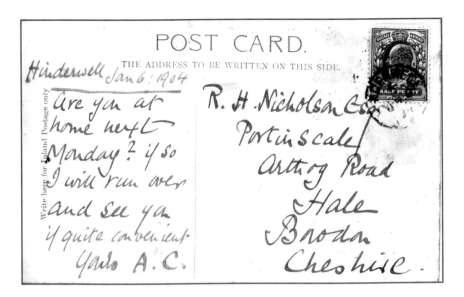

Addressed to:

> R.H. Nicholson Esq
> Portinscale
> Arthog Road
> Hale
> Brodon
> Cheshire

The first thing we can deduce from this card is that the postal service was equally as fast in 1904 as it is today, some may say more so!

Close inspection of the card reveals an artist who can just be seen working on the sand at the far side of the beached coble boats. We must assume this is Arthur Friedenson, commonly known as 'Friedie'.

There is a very strong possibility the sender is Staithes Group artist Andrew Colley (1859–1910) who was known to often stay and paint in Runswick Bay around this time. More interestingly, a cursory check at H.M. Land Registry, reveals that Arthog Road is an extremely expensive location to buy property today, and was likely to be the case in 1904. It is also likely that Mr Nicholson was an important patron to the artists. How difficult it must have been to organise meetings, transport and display work, let alone secure a sale or commission, considerations many of us take for granted today.

Below is a list of core Staithes Group artists mentioned in this diary:

William Frederick Mayor 1866–1916
Arthur Friedenson 1872–1955
Thomas Barrett ARE 1845–1924
Joseph Richard Bagshawe RBA 1870–1909
Dame Laura Knight (née Johnson) DBE, RA, RWS, RE. 1877–1970
Robert Jobling 1841–1923
Isa Jobling (née Thompson) 1851–1926
Harold Knight RA, ROI., RP 1874V1961
Frank Henry Mason RBA, RI 1875–1965
Ernest Higgins Rigg 1868–1947
Frederick Stuart Richardson RSW, RI, ROI 1855–1934

Other lesser known artists contained herein:

Alfred Rigg (younger brother of Ernest Higgins Rigg) 1870–1919
Frank Hillyard Swinstead 1862–1937 (younger brother of George
Hillyard Swinstead RBA (1860–1926)) Headmaster at Hornsey
College of Art and a first class cricket player from 1888–1900
(Gentlemen of England and Marylebone Cricket Club).
William Todd Brown RA, ROI, RI 1875–1952 studied at the Slade
School under Philip Wilson Steer & Professor Henry Tonks.
Rosaline Good 1868–1931(student of Laura Johnson), married to
Irish sculptor Oliver Sheppard.

Runswick Bay, The Cock Pit. *(Two artists are at work in the foreground).*

In Summary

A further book is under consideration and research into the main characters and events is currently underway, not least the identity of 'D'. This investigative work is likely to take some time, consequently, due to the numerous requests to read the diary and our hope that further information may come to light, it was thought best to release the diary immediately. Could I once again reiterate our appeal for any information, especially regarding the source of this diary.

Other Sources of Historical Information and Background Literature

No visit to Staithes is complete without taking in the Staithes Heritage Centre and the Captain Cook Museum. Housed in the old Primitive Methodist Chapel, the Centre and Museum fills two floors. The ground floor houses extensive displays of the lives of the past residents of Staithes with particular reference to the Fishing Industry, whilst the upper floor is crammed with literally hundreds, if not thousands, of exhibits from the life and voyages of Captain James Cook. This is a privately funded museum and there is a small entrance fee. Telephone 01947 841454 for opening times.

Some of the material below may be out of print and only available from specialist book sellers found on the internet.

PHOTOGRAPHIC

Richardson, G. *T Watson Photographer of Lythe, Near Whitby*. Lampada Press, 1992.

Hiley, Michael. *Frank Sutcliffe: Photographer of Whitby*. Phillimore & Co Ltd, 2005.

Bullamore, Colin. *Ross, Photographer, Whitby – The life and work of a Yorkshire artist*. 2010.

Cook, Robin. *Teeside and Old Cleveland Through Time*. Amberley Publishing, 2010.

YORKSHIRE COAST HISTORY

Frank, Peter. *Yorkshire Fisherfolk*. Phillimore & Co Ltd, 2002.

Johnson, J S. *The Nagars of Runswick Bay*. Published 1973, 1985 and 1992.

Graves, Rev. *The History of Cleveland*. F.Jollie & Sons, 1808.

STAITHES HISTORY

Eccleston, J. & Eccleston, P. *The History & Geology of Staithes*. 1998.

Howard, John. *Staithes, Chapters from the History of a Seafaring Town*. 2000.

Brown, Jane & Croden, Ian. *Staithes*. 1977.

Clark, David. *Between Pulpit and Pew, Folk Religion in a North Yorkshire Village*. Cambridge University Press, 1982.

STAITHES GROUP ARTIST REFERENCE CATALOGUES AND BOOKS

Phillips, Peter. *The Staithes Group*. Phillips and Sons, 1993.

Jordan, Rosamund & Wood, Simon. *Staithes Group Centenary Exhibition*. 2003.

Haworth, Peter. *Paintings by Members of the Staithes Group*. 2002.

Haworth, Peter. *From Runswick to Russia*. 2005.

Millard, John. *A Romance with the North-East – Robert and Isa Jobling*. T&WM, 1992.

Dunbar, Janet. *Laura Knight*. William Collins & Co. Ltd, 1975.

Fox, Caroline. *Dame Laura Knight*. Phaidon, Oxford, 1988.

Lübbren, Nina. *Rural Artists' Colonies in Europe 1870–1910*. Rutgers University Press, 2001.

BIOGRAPHICAL HISTORY

Knight, Laura. *Oil Paint and Grease Paint (First Volume)*, (autobiography). 1936.

Knight, Laura. *The Magic of a Line* (autobiography). William Kimber, 1965.

HISTORICAL FICTION

The late 19th century novels of Whitby authoress, Mary Linskill (alias Stephen Yorke), particularly *In Exchange for a Soul* and *The Haven Under the Hill*.

Taylor, Amanda. *The Chinaman's Bastard*. Vanguard Press, 2009.

Books marked in bold text have been used as a source of information herein.

A Missing Painting

In Honor's introduction, you will remember her mentioning a painting which I have since found out hung in her family home at Felix House, Middleton St George, County Durham. Enid married a Doctor Stanley Steavenson, and they both ran a Tubercolosis Sanatorium in the grounds of the property. In the mid 1970s the painting was stolen after it had been cut from the stretcher and the frame broken.

Honor is very modest in not saying that she too inherited her mother's artistic ability, still painting in watercolours and holding exhibitions with her art group. She then went on to tell me how upsetting it was for her when this family heirloom was lost and still wonders of its whereabouts. So much so, and not being one to let such a loss affect her, she set about recreating the painting. She managed to find an old black and white

interior photograph which showed the painting in the background, which she then used as a reference along with her memory to paint the copy oil painting you see here. I have compared the two and they are almost identical in detail except for scale, Honor's being much smaller. The original painting was one of two commissioned for the Sisters, Lucy and Katherine, and painted by the artist 'Harold Begbie', measuring approximately 3ft wide by 4ft high out of its 1ft gilt frame.

Have you seen this painting?